THIS IS RAGTIME

THIS IS RACTIME

BY TERRY WALDO

WITH A FOREWORD BY **Eubie Blake**

New introduction by the author

A DA CAPO PAPERBACK

Library of Congress Cataloging in Publication Data

Waldo, Terry.
  This is ragtime / by Terry Waldo; with a foreword by Eubie Blake.
      p.   cm. —(A Da Capo paperback)
  Includes bibliographical references.
  Discography: p.
  ISBN 0-306-80439-5
  1. Ragtime music — History and criticism. I. Title.
[ML3530.W34   1991   90-27393
781.64—dc20   CIP
                                                                           MN

This Da Capo Press paperback edition of Terry Waldo's *This Is Ragtime*
is an unabridged republication of the edition published in New York
in 1976, here supplemented with a new introduction by the author.
It is reprinted by arrangement with the author.

Published by Da Capo Press, Inc.
A Subsidiary of Plenum Publishing Corporation
233 Spring Street, New York, N.Y. 10013

Manufactured in the United States of America

INTRODUCTION TO THE PAPERBACK EDITION

As we left our story in 1976 the Scott Joplin craze was beginning to diminish. Yet in 1990 Joplin still survives, though hardly a central figure in the mass media. His opera, *Treemonisha*, has had no recent performances, but his name is in most classical music racks at the record stores along with Bach and Beethoven. Sadly, there is very little available that reflects the pre-1970s interpretations before the music was "classicized" to death.

The greatest loss to ragtime was the passing of Eubie Blake. Eubie, unquestionably the key figure in the most recent revival of the music, capped off a miraculous life and died on February 12, 1983, five days after a glorious celebration of his 100th birthday. During his last decade I had the good fortune to be his protégé, spending a great deal of time in concert and on tour with him.

We also lost several younger members of the ragtime community including Dick Wellstood, Turk Murphy, Lu Watters and Johnny Guarnieri. Unfortunately I omitted Guarnieri's name in the original book because I thought of him primarily as a jazz piano player. He was in fact an astounding ragtime musician, having written numerous rags and performed his own highly original arrangements (often in 5/4) of such classics as the "Maple Leaf Rag."

There have been a number of talented and inventive new players and composers of ragtime. These include, among others, David Thomas Roberts, Morton Gunnar Larsen, and violinist David Refkin.

There are, likewise, a number of new ragtime ensembles of all sorts that have surfaced since 1976. Noted among these is the Red Rose Ragtime Band with Joan Reynolds and Joe Cavalier.

Many small record labels have attempted to make ragtime available, but the hands-down leader in the field is Bob Erdos, whose Stomp Off Records (549 Fairview Terrace, York, PA. 17403) has put out more ragtime albums in the last ten years than all others combined. I have recorded eight albums for Erdos. Much of my work has also been re-released by Musical Heritage Society (1710 Highway 35, Ocean, NJ. 07712).

I have also been composing and performing with Leon Redbone, to all appearances the only current popular entertainer whose music has a real ragtime feel to it.

Finally, a special note of recognition to my singing partner, Susan LaMarche, who helped put this book together in 1976 and since has recorded a number of ragtime songs that capture the sound and spirit of the ragtime era perfectly.

I have listed only a few of the many people who are still keeping the music alive and fresh in spite of the mass media's total indifference. Thank God for them all.

Terry Waldo
New York City
September, 1990

To Eubie and Marion Blake,
whose friendship has meant so much to me.

Contents

Cover of the first complete transcriptions of Eubie Blake's rags, published in 1975, compiled by Terry Waldo.

Foreword

The first time I met Terry Waldo was in 1969 at the St. Louis Ragtime Festival on the Goldenrod Showboat. At that time he was one of the very few people who played my "Charleston Rag." He was a good pianist but he was struggling. Since then he's hit the top—he has become not only a fine musician but also an excellent entertainer. I want to emphasize this. The first time I ever heard Terry play the "12th Street Rag" I died laughing! In all my years in show business I've found out that that's one of the hardest things to do—make people laugh. Terry's ability to do this, combined with his musicianship, actually reminds me of Fats Waller! Now, I'm not going to say that I taught Terry how to play, because he already knew his stuff when I met him. But during the eight years we've known each other Terry has spent a lot of time with me learning *my* music and learning about the people I have known and the way we used to live and perform. I mean that what Terry has learned from me is not so much the notes but the history, the tricks, the attitudes, the *essence* of ragtime.

It's not the same as it used to be. Anyone can learn the notes, and that's how they play it today: They play *the* notes—but that's not ragtime. Ragtime is *syncopation* and *improvisation* and *accents*. We all played our own style, but if you could have heard those old fellas play, you would have heard ad lib and those accents. Though seldom written into the music, they're very important, but you just don't hear them any more.

Recently Terry transcribed and edited a folio of my rags called *Sincerely, Eubie Blake*. This is the first time anyone has done this. I never could have done all that work myself, and I want to take the opportunity in print to say how grateful I am.

Terry knows about this music as few others do, for the music itself is only a part of it. You have to know about the backrooms of bars, the incredible prejudice we had to deal with, the hook shops, the beer and sawdust all over the floor; but these were the only places you could hear Jesse Pickett, Jack the Bear, Boots Butler. You have to understand the background; you can't pretend it has nothing to do with ragtime.

I heard ragtime all my life and it was cried down, even by the upper-class Negroes. But I always knew it was good music. Likewise, Terry's love of ragtime goes back a long way, long before its "rediscovery." People then were always trying to talk him out of playing that "corny old stuff," telling him that he'd never go anywhere with it. But he knew it was good music, too. And he knows, as I've said, that there's much more to it than just the notes. Not everyone playing ragtime today realizes that. Or they try to modernize it with lots of meaningless ad lib and end up losing the melody.

When I was young there were no books on ragtime or how to play it even though it had already been going on a long time. Now nearly everyone who used to know about it is dead, and *been* dead for many years, except me. Terry's a fine pianist, but that's not what makes him qualified to write this book. What it is is that he's always asked a lot of questions, the *right* questions, and he's been sharp enough to understand the answers. I believe Terry has written the *real* story on ragtime.

EUBIE BLAKE

Acknowledgments

My research on the subject of this book actually has been going on for about twenty years, since I first became interested in ragtime, so there is an enormous number of people who have contributed, directly or indirectly, to the creation of this book. Obviously I cannot mention them all, but I would like to thank as many as I can remember who have been particularly helpful.

Throughout the book you will find extensive quotes. Some are documented in footnotes; the ones that are not have been taken directly from personal interviews. The following persons graciously provided those interviews between the years of 1972 and 1976: Paul E. Bierley, Eubie Blake, Rudi Blesh, William Bolcom, Lou Busch (Joe "Fingers" Carr), Robert Darch, David Jasen, Amelia Lamb, Vera Brodsky Lawrence, John Maddox, Chink Martin, Max Morath, Turk Murphy, Frank Powers, Joshua Rifkin, Wally Rose, Gunther Schuller, Mildred Marshall Steward, Lu Watters, and Dick Wellstood.

I would like also to thank the many folk who kindly allowed me to pick their skulls and resources concerning their particular fields of expertise, including Samuel and Ann Charters, Pete Clute, Jim Dapogny, Phil Elwood, Tony Hoggart, Lew Green, Bob Helm, Jim and Martha Hession, Leslie Carole Johnson, Wayne Jones, Edward Lawless, Mike Lipskin, Peter Lundberg, Allen and Idamay MacInnes, Gene Mayl, Larry Melton, Jim Messina, Mike

Montgomery, Bill Moorhead, Isabelle Sayers, Carl Seltzer, Ed Sprankle, Butch Thompson, Trebor Jay Tichenor, Ian Whitcomb, Bob Wright, and Dick Zimmerman.

Special acknowledgment goes to Addison Reed, Jr., for his contribution of Scott Joplin information prior to the publication of his own book; to Joe Scotti, likewise, for the use of his materials on Joe Lamb; to David Jansen for the major portion of the Discography; to Al Rose who gave so generously of his time and resources, enabling me to do quite a bit of my research in New Orleans; to Tulane University and Richard Allen of the William Ransom Hogan Jazz Archive who also provided much needed assistance.

Finally, I would like to express my gratitude to those close friends who furnished me with feedback, services of various kinds, and direction for the book. Among these my editor, Sandra Choron, who put up with my madness longer than humanly possible; Barbi Herman, who read the manuscript and offered much needed moral support; John (Jack) Baker for graciously allowing me unlimited access to his vast jazz-film collection; to Marcia Hulen for the transcription and beautiful calligraphy on the musical illustrations; to Mildred Steward for allowing, for the first time, the publication of "Little Jack's Rag" (by her father, Arthur Marshall).

THIS IS RAGTIME

1
The Roots of Ragtime

WHAT IS RAGTIME?

Only ten years ago, when most people thought of ragtime, the word conjured up images of tinny, out-of-tune pianos and straw hats. It was that corny music from beer halls and pizza parlors, that happy music that people sang along with. Then in the 1970s general audiences discovered Scott Joplin, and ragtime was suddenly moved from the saloon to the concert hall. Within a few years the gentle, haunting melodies of this black musical genius were introduced first to the classical music devotees of Joshua Rifkin and then to the public at large through the sound track of the very popular film *The Sting*. Here, then, is an amazing phenomenon: The king of ragtime, Scott Joplin, whose fine composition the "Maple Leaf Rag" had launched what is popularly called the ragtime era in 1899, is totally forgotten by the general public, then emerges once again some seventy years later with enormous hits on both the classical and popular music charts.

The question may come to mind, What is ragtime? Is it classical music, as Joplin himself called it, or is it popular music? Or is it something else entirely? It seems to defy precise musical definition. In many minds ragtime is considered a primitive form of jazz, in others a type of folk music. Ragtime is in fact all of these things and much more. Its roots extend far back into the last century, encompassing every musical source available in America, and it has influenced in some way almost every type of American music that has evolved since. It is America's first and most unique contribution to musical literature.

Like the very slippery term *jazz*, *ragtime* almost has to be defined operationally; that is, it is best defined by what types of music are included in the term. As we shall see, this forms a wide and constantly changing body of music. The conception of ragtime that has emerged in the 1970s is in fact completely different from any previous ideas about it. We have not witnessed in this decade a simple revival of ragtime but a reassessment of the music in terms of our day. The same may be said of all ragtime revivals that have occurred over the past thirty or so years. *Ragtime* for Scott Joplin did not mean the same thing as it means for Marvin Hamlisch or Joshua Rifkin.

This book attempts to relate some idea of what a great many people think of as ragtime and explores some of the creative efforts that have borne the label over the past eighty-odd years. Also, in some cases, I have included musical ideas that may not have been called ragtime per se but seem to fit the spirit of the music. Probably the best way to begin is to make a distinction between a rag and ragtime.

A *rag*, strictly speaking, is an instrumental, syncopated march and follows the same formal conventions as the march. *Ragtime*, however, is a much more eclectic term and could be said to apply to almost any music that is syncopated. To *rag* a number is to play it in a syncopated style. So ragtime encompasses not only the instrumental rags but also such diverse musical forms as the rag song and Dixieland.

Although no one now living seems to know for sure the original meaning of the word *ragtime*, it seems to have come from the phrase *ragged time*—tearing time apart. But there are several other possible derivations. For instance, the term *to rag* at one time meant "to tease," and the music does just that—it teases the listener. It's full of surprises—unexpected rhythmic shifts and harmonies. Whatever its origin, however, we know that by the mid-1890s the word was applied to a wide variety of music that had this common element of syncopation.

Syncopation is the continuous superimposition of an irregular rhythm overtop of a regular one. In the piano rags a regular pulse is maintained by the left hand alternating a low bass note with a chord in the midrange. This produces a heavy accent on the first and third beats of the measure. Pitted against this regular meter is a constant series of rhythmic displacements in the right hand. In band or orchestra ragtime the functions of the left and right hands are taken over by various instruments.

Although syncopation is essentially of African origin, its combination with the European musical system accounts for the essential uniqueness of ragtime. This was the first significant musical innovation to evolve from the cultural interchange brought about by slavery in the United States. And so ragtime is, at least in its inception, Afro-American music.

Ragtime as we know it today is composed within the European written framework. This means a notational system based on measures and divisions of measures. We think in terms of half notes and quarter notes. A time signature indicates how many beats will be in a measure and what kind of note receives one beat. As an example: In ¾ time, which is waltz time, there are three beats per measure and a quarter note receives one beat. A half note would receive two beats. Each note is conceived of as a division of the measure.

However African music is based on an entirely different frame of reference. First, it is not notated. It is transmitted aurally, that is, learned by hearing. Second, the music is polyrhythmic. Unlike European music, African music gives at least as much emphasis to rhythm (instruments without pitch, such as drums) as it does to melody and harmony. Consequently, much of African music contains very sophisticated and complicated polyrhythmic patterns. Typically, one drummer would establish a primary pulse in duple or triple time, then other rhythmic instruments would set up various rhythmic patterns overtop of this basic pulse. This is essentially an *additive* process as opposed to the *divisive* European system. Many African drummers are able to play polyrhythms alone—one rhythm with one hand and a separate pattern with the other—and this has been to some extent transferred to ragtime in rather diluted form. Commonly called secondary rag, it most often appears in ragtime as duple meter coinciding with triple meter. In pure African music the two separate meters would be given equal weight, actual polyrhythm. However, using a Western notational system, one pattern must take dominance, the other becoming an irregular pattern.

Euday Bowman's "12th Street Rag" is typical. It is written as:

but it might be more properly thought of as:

Another important African musical element in ragtime is the emphasis on the percussiveness of the music. This results in a great variety and subtlety of accents. Unfortunately our European notational system is biased toward harmony, melody, and rhythm; accents are an essential ingredient in ragtime but quite difficult to notate properly.

It should also be pointed out that the African influence is seen in the melodic and harmonic structures of ragtime. Although based on the traditional European major and minor scales, much of the music belies a preference for the pentatonic scale, which is more prevalent in African music.*

We can think of all of these contrasts in purely musical terms, but I think the fundamental differences in the two musical heritages go even deeper than that. There is so much of African music that does not translate into European terms because of the cultural difference in the function and conception of music. In African societies there is no separation between the artist (musician) and the audience. Everyone participates in the musical event through dancing, singing, or playing. And the music is not simply what is heard, it is the whole performance. Gestures and movements are just as important as the sounds.

---

* A pentatonic scale may be achieved by using only the black keys on a piano.

The European musical tradition tends to isolate these various participants and functions. The artist (performer/composer) creates a musical product for a quite separate audience. This product often is transmitted through the medium of *notated* music, and therefore a great deal of emphasis is placed on the written note rather than the total live performance that is so much a part of the Afro-American musical tradition. This is roughly the difference between *classical* music and *folk* music; and this is where ragtime sits: straddling the fence between the two.

RAGTIME FOLK SOURCES

The uneasy position that ragtime occupies in the musical world reflects the overall situation of blacks in this country, and the roots of ragtime extend as far back as our institution of slavery—we could say roughly to the year 1700, for by then that institution had become firmly established throughout the thirteen colonies.

The nature of early Afro-American music varied from locale to locale, but generally these slaves, who were barred from performing pure African music, were instead performing European music in African styles. This means that all of the musical source material available to them would have been improvised upon and often syncopated. Blacks in performance were transforming this material into new compositions and actually developing new styles of playing in the process.

In spite of the fact that there were from the beginning a number of free blacks, the large body of Afro-American music still came from the slaves and was pure folk music in that it evolved from the daily life of the people. Most of it falls into one of three categories: religious music, dance music, and work songs.

Perhaps the most important musical outlet for the slaves was religious music. Especially in the North, whites were concerned about the spiritual uplifting of the slaves and so in many cases permitted them to attend religious services (although usually in separate sections of the churches). Over the years blacks modified certain hymns and added their own lyrics. The result was the spiritual.

A number of spirituals came out of the Great Awakening, a revival movement that began around 1780 and lasted until about

1830. This was essentially an interracial phenomenon in which the various Protestant denominations would hold services, sometimes lasting several days at a time, in tents in the woods. The camp meetings, as they were called, took on special significance for blacks because they became an outlet for the expression of the African musical tradition. Written hymn texts were of little use to the largely illiterate crowds assembled in the weak light of a campfire, and so the religious leaders led the singing with easy-to-follow phrases—parts of hymns, prayers, and religious exhortations often made up on the spot.

The camp meetings also employed a rather pure African form of dancing known as the ring shout. At camp meetings and bush meetings (camp meetings without tents) the crowds would form large circles, singing spirituals, clapping their hands, and dancing in a shuffling movement. These camp meetings and ring shouts lasted beyond slavery into the twentieth century and, as we shall see, directly influenced a variety of ragtime composers.

The instrumental antecedents of ragtime would seem to have come from the musicians of the plantations, who entertained not only the slaves but also their masters. By 1800 a number of Negroes had established themselves as dance accompanists and musical entertainers, and there was a great demand for these self-taught artists.

The most common instruments used for the dance music were handmade fiddles and banjos. They were usually unfretted and often made out of large gourds. Musical expertise was most often picked up through observation, though there were instances of formal training. Every plantation had at least one fiddle player who could play the lively jigs and reels for the slaves to dance to and also the more formal minuets, schottisches, and cotillions for the masters. For this reason the musicians were usually considered valuable possessions by their masters.

The plantation dances generally took place on special occasions, such as the annual corn-shucking jubilees. Typically, a farmer would invite his friends and their slaves to help shuck the corn from his fields. The husking would be accompanied by a great deal of singing, followed by a feast. Then the fiddler or banjo player (or sometimes even a small group of players) would play for the dancers for most of the night.

After the Civil War hundreds of these musicians wandered the country picking up work wherever they could and exchanging musical ideas in the process. This army of itinerant folk musicians had a strong influence on early ragtime, especially in the Midwest and South.

Although slave work songs are generally considered to be primary sources for blues and not ragtime, I think a case could be made that the vocal style of the work songs influenced all black music, including ragtime. The melancholy emotional intensity of the songs can be detected in many of the rags, and, according to many of the old-timers, a number of ragtime melodies can be traced directly to these vocal songs.

The work-song melodies were often based on the major or pentatonic scale, but there is evidence to suggest that in actual singing there was a slight lowering of certain pitches, producing a melancholy cast to most of the music. These would most likely be the notes we have commonly called "blue" notes, the slightly flatted third and seventh notes of a major scale. Though not as prevalent in ragtime as in jazz, the ragtime players nonetheless put these dissonant blue notes into their music.

Many work songs and Negro dances were disseminated by blacks who were employed as stevedores along the eastern seaboard; the Gulf coast; and the Mississippi, Ohio, and Missouri rivers. Fifty or so of these men would travel with each boat and load and unload the cargo. Reports give evidence that they generally worked under terrible conditions, but the men sang as they worked and danced when there was nothing to do. Their improvised music found its way all up and down the various waterways of the United States and can be shown to have been a direct influence on the rag writers. The earliest rags often displayed on their covers pictures of the laborers dancing on the levee, and several themes from the rags came directly from the folk songs of these roustabouts. An excellent example of one of these tunes is "Buddy Bolden's Blues." It was attributed to Buddy Bolden, the legendary New Orleans trumpeter, but elsewhere it appeared with the title "I Thought I Heard Judge Fogerty Say." It was incorporated into several rags, most notably the "St. Louis Tickle" by Barney and Seymour in 1904.

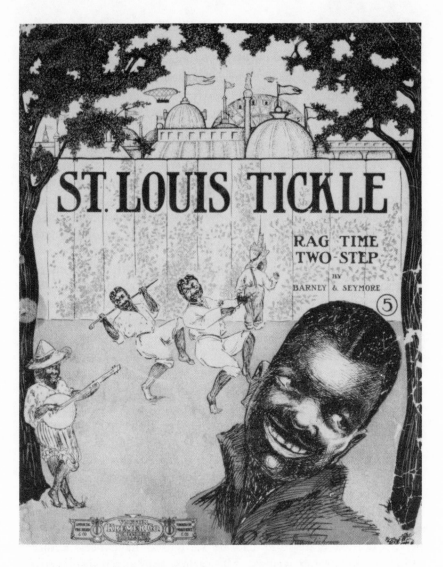

A folk song turned rag. Courtesy of Trebor Tichenor.

MINSTREL SHOWS

In all of these various folk sources we can see a fairly pure expression of Afro-American sentiments, whether they be the religious fervor of the spiritual, the sensual joy of the dance, or the pathos and hardship of the work song. This was black music intended to be experienced by blacks. However, ragtime, when it finally emerged, was not directed primarily at blacks but rather at white audiences. It drew from the Afro-American folk sources, but it drew even more heavily from the theatrical music of the minstrel shows.

The minstrel show is America's first and probably only native theatrical art form. Its antecedents date back to before the 1830s when it was common for many southern plantations to have small bands of black entertainers who would present shows that would include jokes, dancing, and songs to the accompaniment of banjo and bones, which were used as rhythm instruments, much in the manner of castanets. The members of these semiprofessional groups were not musicians per se but were more like improvising clowns. Music was only a part of their bag of tricks.

Beginning in the early 1830s professional white entertainers began to copy these plantation showmen. Thomas "Daddy" Rice, who may justifiably be called the father of stage minstrelsy, first introduced his "Jim Crow" in 1832. This Negro caricature was created from observing the "eccentric" dancing and personal mannerisms of an old black stable hand. The act was first presented at the Bowery Theater in New York City. It was a tremendous success and launched the whole minstrelsy movement, which reached its height around 1870. At that time the entertainment could be described as a healthy blend of sturdy, clean comedy and pleasant, if somewhat diluted, Negro folk music.

The form of the minstrel show was perfected by the very popular Edwin Christy Minstrels. In the standard version a smartly dressed "Mr. Interlocutor" would sit in the center of the stage and function as the master of ceremonies. He would be surrounded by a semicircle of chorus members in blackface, who played tambourines. The "end men" were Mr. Bones to the far left and Mr. Tambo on the far right. Each was named for his respective instrument, of course, which was usually soloed at some time during the performance. The end men would also throw jokes back and forth with the aid of Mr. Interlocutor and full choric support from the other members. This jolly opening would then be followed by what was called the "olio," which was a forerunner to the variety shows of a later era. The performance would conclude with everyone participating in a giant "walk around."

Unfortunately the period of 1875 to 1895 saw an artistic decline and simultaneous increased popularity of the minstrel shows; in short, commercialism triumphed. This has been called by musicologists the Second Age of Minstrelsy, following the first Golden Age, which lasted from 1842 to 1875.

By this time any attempt at a faithful representation of the subtle humor of the Negro in song, movement, and speech was a thing of the past. In the Second Age the near-genuine article was replaced with heavy-handed caricatures and tacky stereotypes. This was the age of the circus mentality, and the P. T. Barnum dictates of playing down to the crowds were rapidly gaining momentum.

During this period the comic image of the happy-go-lucky, wide-grinnin', chicken-stealin', razor-totin' darky became rigidly embedded in the psyche of white America. And from this tradition came a flood of pseudo-Negro entertainment that persisted throughout the ragtime era. Even black performers, who became actively involved in the traveling shows after the Civil War, were forced to don the burnt cork in order to darken their complexions and to portray caricatures of themselves. The minstrel shows nonetheless provided work opportunities for blacks in the entertainment field, opportunities for which they were grateful in those difficult times. There were at least three Negro-owned and -operated troups, and many important black ragtime and jazz musicians traveled with them.

From all accounts the shows provided a creative, earthy atmosphere for the entertainer. The show people took care of one another, took pride in their musicianship, and worked hard to present new material and original arrangements. In addition, although few acts were racially integrated, many of these shows did employ both blacks and whites and thereby provided an opportunity for musical cross-pollination. But they remained at least one step removed from the Negro folk roots.

It is difficult for us now to realize how all-pervasive and influential the minstrel show was. Music publishers turned out prepackaged shows that amateur church groups could perform; hundreds of professionals toured the country; and in later years the "darky syndrome" permeated all other forms of entertainment as well (including movies and records). Vaudeville was a direct descendant of the olio of the minstrel show, and the grand walk, or walk around, became the cakewalk craze that swept the United States in the 1890s.

THE MARCH

An important tradition of the minstrel-show era was the "11:45" A.M. parade and concert, during which the entire cast, including the band, would march through town playing the popular marches of the day as promotion for the evening show. Military marches were extremely popular throughout the 1890s. This was a time when America was beginning to flex her military muscles and think of herself as the strongest nation on earth. John Philip Sousa, an eminently practical entertainer, captured this nationalistic fever and made the march an American institution. He was so successful that by early 1900 he was considered the most popular musician in the world.*

Although Sousa's numbers were patterned after older German marches, they were not as complicated. They were buoyant, optimistic, overtly physical, patriotic, and above all easily understandable by the public. But Sousa's organization was more than just a marching band. He pioneered the concept of the concert band. Filled with many of the top musicians in the country, Sousa's band was capable of playing everything from the pop tunes of the day, such as "After the Ball," to the great European masterworks. Moreover his marches, beginning in 1889 with "The Washington Post," were used by dancing masters for the new two-step, which was to replace the waltz as the popular ballroom dance of the day.

Sousa's influence over America's music was immense. While he crisscrossed the country for years playing to standing-room-only crowds, his compositions were also played by local bands. And among these were a number of all-black groups that infused the marches with African syncopation. Eubie Blake, who was composing rags before the turn of the century, recalls hearing these bands as a child in Baltimore: "I used to hear the colored bands going to the funerals. On the way over they'd play the funeral march straight, but coming back they'd rag the hell out of the music. So I started playing my music like that." From all indications this was the common practice in most major cities of the United States with a sizable black population.

---

*Paul Bierly, *John Philip Sousa: American Phenomenon* (Englewood Cliffs, N.J.: Prentice-Hall, 1973), p. 7.

CULTURAL CENTERS

It is fairly simple to pick out several musical factors, national in scope, that influenced ragtime—the folk-music traditions of blacks, the minstrel shows, and the marching bands. In addition to these, however, there were musical and social influences peculiar to individual sections of the country. These places were generally the centers of commerce, where blacks could get work in the tenderloin districts that invariably developed with the financial growth of a city. But there was also, in some cities, a good amount of "high culture" available to blacks, and this greatly influenced their musical activity as well.

In the North one of the earliest and most influential cultural centers was New York. At the beginning of the nineteenth century New York was already the artistic mecca of the United States. As early as 1821 the free slaves of the city maintained their own theater, the African Globe, where ballets and plays were given by black performers. At the same time there was also an antecedent to the Harlem district of the 1920s. This was an area called the Five Points. It was the refuge for newly freed slaves and working-class whites. As such it was one of the worst slums in the United States at the time, but from all indications (including a reference by Charles Dickens in 1842*) the dance halls there swung with the music of primitive ragtime or jazz. So we see in New York quite early two trends that would continue for years: a theatrical establishment that would come to dominate all others in the United States and a black "hot" music emanating from the notorious slums of the city. Other northern cultural centers included Boston and Philadelphia, where there are reports of ragtime, or jig piano, as it was called, as early as 1875.

In the South the greatest cultural center was undoubtedly New Orleans. This was the first city in the United States to have a permanent opera company, and there were, as well, concerts of all sorts, plays, balls, street parades, and, of course, the exciting Mardi Gras celebration.

New Orleans at the time of the Louisiana Purchase in 1803 could be considered the true melting pot of the United States.

---

* Charles Dickens, *American Notes* (London: Oxford University Press, 1957).

French, German, Spanish, English, Irish, and African traditions combined to form an "American" culture. There was, however, a rigid racial caste system separating whites, Afro-Americans, and "Creoles of color." The members of this last group were descendants of the black mistresses of early French and Spanish settlers in New Orleans, and they took great pride in their European cultural associations.

In contrast to the racially mixed Creoles, the slaves and freedmen had direct African ties. In fact, Congo Square, during the first half of the nineteenth century, was one of the few places in the United States where it was possible to hear pure African music. Slaves representing six African tribes could be seen there on Sunday afternoons engaged in so-called wild dancing, singing, and playing to the accompaniment of such instruments as drums, crude banjos, rattles, and the like. It is difficult to estimate the actual influence of this music, but it must have been great, especially among the Negro population. Although city officials stopped the festivals in 1843, the music survived in underground form in taverns and other nightspots, and the dances became part of the religious ring shouts. More important, the African music was eventually infused into the conventional band music that was extremely popular in New Orleans. This is the beginning of what we have come to call jazz.

There are many theories as to how this music actually developed, but the most significant single event in its evolution seems to have been the appearance of a Mexican band at the Sugar and Cattle Exposition held in New Orleans in 1885. It is reported by many older musicians that this group had a profound effect on New Orleans music. It not only inspired a younger generation of would-be musicians by the quality of its performance, but on a more practical level, it supplied necessary musical equipment to a number of players: After their extremely successful engagement the Mexican musicians found that they could profit by selling their instruments in New Orleans and replacing them later in Mexico. So in the wake of their visit they left a plethora of inexpensive horns in the hands of dozens of enthusiastic children.

These kids had little or no acquaintance with music theory, yet, managing after a fashion to master the technical intricacies of the instruments, they often were able to achieve beautiful tone colors. And in their attempts to imitate the music they had heard, they usually ended up incorporating elements of African music as well. The net result was jazz—but they called it ragtime first!

From all indications, early ragtime bands were quite a rag-tag affair. Chink Martin, an aging New Orleans bass and tuba player, recently described the first groups to me as he remembered them:

> If you heard them now, you'd laugh yourself to death. None of them could read, and they knew nothing about music theory. You know the slide trombone? Well, they started using that down here because the guy could start down at the end, slide up, and then stop when he found the right note! They were so bad you couldn't tell what tune they were playing until they got into the third chorus.

During the 1890s there were probably 150 or so of these primitive jazz or ragtime bands playing in New Orleans. Each group consisted of six or seven pieces for dances, expanding to more for parades. Musicians were generally interchangeable, and such entrepreneurs as Jack Laine, who dominated the business, would often have several bands out at the same time.

The type of tunes generally played were simple sixteen-bar songs, often made up on the spot, or standard marches, such as "Stars and Stripes Forever," which were often faked. Jack Laine once said, "If you syncopate a march, you have a rag." Actually, though, he was referring more directly to the origin of jazz than to that of ragtime. Both types of music used the same folk-music sources, but ragtime as we think of it became more of a composed music of longer form, whereas jazz music from its beginnings emphasized spontaneous improvisation. Ragging a tune in the way these New Orleans boys were doing was really different from playing a rag. Nonetheless, the influence of that music was important in the development of ragtime.

THE ARTS

The most far-reaching trend in the nineteenth century in the "legitimate" music of the United States was the so-called genteel tradition. Following the Civil War the reaction of most of our writers and composers was to retreat from reality and turn to the escapism of romantic imagery. Starting with the assumption that American society was basically vulgar and materialistic and believing all American art to be an inferior brand of European art, those who dominated the artistic establishment used all of their influence to suppress any form of artistic expression that even faintly suggested realism. Superficial bits and pieces of European art, past and present, were glorified under the catch-all term *classicism;* and any potentially vital form of American art was violently attacked or emasculated. Sex and social reform were purged from novels; functionalism was downgraded in architecture; and the art music of the day reeked with flowery ornaments and drippy sentiment totally divorced from everyday life. American artists were sent to Europe to study with the great masters, and very few of them could come away from the experience without having been overwhelmed by their teachers. Certainly the white musical artists of the day generally failed to do so.

In contrast to this imitative approach, Afro-American music contained a goldmine of native material, which a number of educated Negro musicians were in a position to develop. Men such as Will Marion Cook, W. C. Handy, and Scott Joplin had the necessary education to be included in the sterile, establishment art group, but they were barred by their color from full participation. Illustrating the point, Eubie Blake recalls the story of "One-Leg Willie" Joseph:

He was a concert pianist. You see, his mother had worked for some rich white people and they came home one day and heard young Willie playing their piano. So they sent him to the Boston Conservatory, where he majored in music. Now, according to what Willie told me, when they had the commencement, he was one of the five top pianists in the class. They had them play in competition in cubicles where they could not be seen by the audience. Well, he won by the audience applause. So he came out—and he was black—and the man that was the head of the panel to give the awards told him, "I'd like to give you first place, but you being a Negro, I can't; I'd lose my job."

When I worked with him [Willie] he was turning the classics into ragtime. He was the most uncanny piano player you ever heard. He had terrific technique. You'd walk into a room and he would be playing; he'd reach up and shake hands and keep right on playing everything with his left hand.

Willie died a few years after Eubie knew him, an embittered man, having made no recordings, having written down none of his music, and self-destroyed through alcohol and hard drugs.*

The reaction of many intellectual Afro-American musicians, however, was to fight for acceptance. And so, they set about to produce "classical" art music based on their own traditions.

The pioneer work in this area had been done by Louis Moreau Gottschalk, one of America's first great concert pianists. He was born in New Orleans in the early part of the nineteenth century, but after having been recognized as a child prodigy, he received extensive musical education in Paris. By his teens he had become good friends with composers such as Chopin and Berlioz and was soon playing concerts all over the United States in brilliant Chopinesque style.

There are conflicting reports as to whether he actually had some African blood. In any case, Gottschalk was greatly influenced by the Negro folk music of the United States, and he incorporated much of it into his music. Two of his pieces are of particular interest: "The Banjo," written in 1855, which contains an imitation of mid-nineteenth-century plantation banjos; and "Bamboula: Danse des Negres," dating from around 1845, which is said to have had its origin in the music of Congo Square, New Orleans.

John William ("Blind") Boone is another nineteenth-century concert pianist who is important in the same respect as Gottschalk. This black artist from Missouri was the first performer to bring the Negro spiritual to the concert stage. During his forty-year career, which began in the early 1880s, Boone would not only play the standard classics of Liszt, Chopin, and Beethoven, but he would also include raggy Negro music. After the first intermission he would say, "Now I'll put the cookies on the lower shelf where everyone can reach them," and he would launch into one of his Negro folk medleys. Two of these were published by Thomas

---

* Robert Kimball and William Bolcom, eds., *Reminiscing with Sissle and Blake* (New York: Viking Press, 1973), p. 46.

B. Allen: "Blind Boone's Southern Rag Medley Number One—Strains from the Alley," and "Number Two—Strains from the Flat Branch." There are also several hand-played piano rolls that Boone made in 1916 that include a camp-meeting medley.

These rolls are extremely interesting because of their complicated syncopation. Boone was able to duplicate, note for note, any performance of music that he heard, even down to the mistakes, so there is some likelihood that his medleys are copies of early piano styles as he heard them in the underground byways of the Mississippi Valley.

I have come up with no documentation as to when Boone began to perform this rag material, but it is my guess that it was before the late 1890s, when the instrumental rag became an established form. His medleys are not in the sixteen-bar march form of the rags but are more loosely connected folk songs—sometimes sixteen bars, but often not. In any case, he did establish a link between Negro folk music and the concert stage, and he was known to have been a friend of Scott Joplin, who was to further cement that connection.

THE CHICAGO FAIR

The most important single event in terms of bringing together all of the various influences on the development of ragtime was the World's Columbian Exposition held in Chicago in 1893. This massive technological-artistic-commercial display demonstrated for the first time what the "New America" was all about. Constructed after the great Chicago fire that demolished much of the city, there were literally miles of new buildings displaying the technological advances of the industrial revolution. The fair signaled the beginning of a new age, an age of speed and invention, yet its "classical" architecture reflected the irony of an artistically backward cultural establishment.

There was also a world of entertainment to be found at the fair: everything from the "primitive" African music of the Dahomian Village—brought intact directly from the "Dark Continent"—to the martial strains of the Sousa band. And for the first time many of the Negroes who would shape a nationalistic movement toward a legitimacy of black folk music were collected in one location.

The Creole Show, the first Negro review to break out of the blackface mold, was playing the fair; there was work for a number of black musicians: W. C. Handy, who had not yet "fathered" the blues, was appearing with Maholy's Minstrels; and somewhere among all the activities of the fair wandered a young Scott Joplin who would in a few years establish his prominence in the ragtime field.

2
The Ragtime Era

As the Gay Nineties began, the industrial technological revolution and its accompanying urbanization and mass commercialization were forcing drastic changes in American life. Ragtime would become a musical reflection of these changes in two separate ways: as entertainment and as art. It can be said that entertainment serves the function of confirming and reinforcing our prejudices; ragtime as entertainment did just that. It was full of the zip and optimism of the new age, and at the same time it seemed to justify the strong white-supremacy sentiments of the times. On a second level, as art, and primarily black art, ragtime reflected the often frustrating reality of Negroes intent upon equality in a new society.

FORERUNNERS OF RAGTIME

Although it was a part of the underground black subculture long before it appeared in print, ragtime was not published until 1896. It was preceded by two related musical fads: the cakewalk and the "coon song," both outgrowths of the minstrel show, which, as we have seen, had become by the 1890s primarily a commercial showcase of racist humor. The "coon song," a main staple of the minstrel show, represented the alarming upsurge in racist thought that occurred around 1890 and accelerated throughout the ragtime era, which lasted approximately until World War I.

The racist segregation laws of the South were given federal legitimacy in 1896 with the Supreme Court decision on the *Plessy v. Ferguson* case. The court upheld a state law separating races on railroads and, by extension, elsewhere. This signaled the opening of a broad attack on blacks on many fronts. Whites, threatened by the Negroes' increasing ambition and integration into hitherto exclusively white realms, enacted various pieces of legislation to institutionalize what had formerly been only segregationist customs. As long as the Negro "knew his place" and remained subservient, there was little friction. But since the Civil War there had been a movement toward more education and better jobs for blacks. Many were making it on their own, and a significant number were becoming involved in the political process. The resistance to these black advancements took many forms. Politically, Negroes were legally deprived of their voting rights; socially, they were separated from whites in most public places. The justification for this white chauvinism was provided by the "scientific" community. Using Darwin's theory of evolution as a base, these men argued that there existed a hierarchy of races with the Nordic people at the top, followed by the Alpines, the Mediterraneans, and so on, descending in order of excellence down to Negroes.

In the South conditions became worse than they had been in the thirty-five years since the Civil War. As the dawn of a new century approached and white supremacy became increasingly oppressive, lynch mobs became common. Years later many of the musicians of the period still recalled the crackdown. Willie "Bunk" Johnson, some time in the 1940s, told a reporter that "discrimination came in 1889. Too much prejustry [*sic*] in the South since then."* From 1889 to 1899 there were at least 1,460 Negroes lynched.

The most immediate effect of this intense racial attack on black musicians was the necessity to adhere to the racial stereotypes that were insisted upon by the brainwashed public. The mass mind needed to be reassured that its relegation of Negroes to a secondary spot in the system was really justified. The music of the times, especially the "coon songs," fulfilled this function.

* Tom Bethell, "The Revival of Bunk Johnson," *Mississippi Rag*, July 1975, p. 1.

Sheet music cover for 1901 "coon" song. Photograph by Charles Klamkin. From *Old Sheet Music*, by Marian Klamkin (New York: Hawthorn, 1975).

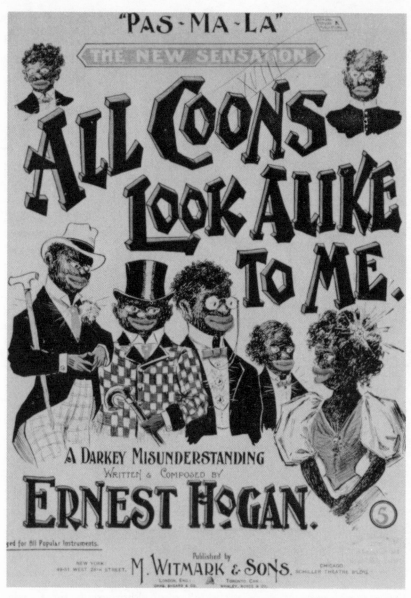

This song actually has innocent lyrics and is not a typical "coon" song. Photograph by Charles Klamkin. From *Old Sheet Music*, by Marian Klamkin (New York: Hawthorn, 1975).

There are several possibilities for the origin of the term *coon* in reference to blacks. One is the contraction of the word *cousin*, which was in common use among blacks in the nineteenth century as a friendly reference, much like *brother*. A second possibility is a connection to the Negro dance, the Counjaille. The most likely source, however, is the animal the raccoon, with its black mask, and the earliest implications of the term were not derogatory; the raccoon was considered a cunning and quick animal. But by the time these songs had reached their height in popularity around 1897, the term had become a degrading, stereotypical appellation. (Pigs are very intelligent animals, too, but you'd hardly find a policeman today willing to be compared.) There were literally thousands of "coon songs" written, based on nothing but minstrel-show images of the black man as lazy, dishonest, cowardly, immoral, vicious, gluttonous, and stupid. "Coon! Coon! Coon!" by Len Friedman and Gene Jefferson, and "If the Man in the Moon Were a Coon," by Fred Fischer, are examples of these.

The cakewalk was a far less offensive form of music than the "coon song"—primarily because it was instrumental music and relied on pure musical energy for its effect. It was a vigorous and exciting dance, and as a musical form, like ragtime, transcended the racial stereotypes that surrounded it. The dance itself is said to have originated as early as 1840 with slaves who dressed up in "high fashion" and mimicked the formal dances of their masters. Their caricatures were picked up by white performers and used in the grand finale of the minstrel shows. Later, after the Civil War, blacks performing in the black-stereotype mold of the white minstrel shows picked up the dance. By the time the ragtime era began in 1896, the cakewalk was being performed by blacks imitating whites who were imitating blacks who were imitating whites.

Although cakewalks were in existence for many years, the first real rise in the popularity of the dance came around 1892. At that time cakewalk extravaganzas were being held all over the country. Couples would compete in local contests, then go to New York for a three-day Cakewalk Jubilee held annually in Madison Square Garden.

The cakewalk fad received its greatest boost from the black comedy-and-song team of Bert Williams and George Walker, who,

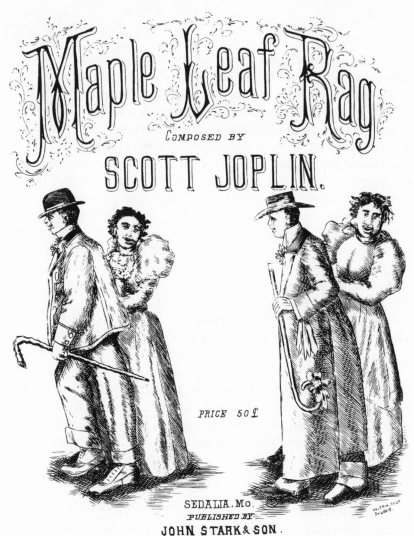

Cover art for the original sheet music of "Maple Leaf Rag"

starting in 1898 with *Clorindy, or The Origin of the Cakewalk*, starred in a number of all-black shows that featured the dance. Pictures of them high-stepping appear in a lithograph on the original cover of Scott Joplin's "Maple Leaf Rag."

As we have seen, the cakewalk was traditionally the grand finale of a show. Dressed in fine clothes, each couple would march in, two by two, doing the high-stepping strut. Then the couples would take turns making up their own variations. At the conclusion they would again high-step in a circle and then file out. Theatrical devices were often employed to enhance the effect; as early as 1893 a flickering kinetoscope was used, much like the strobe light of today, to make the dancers appear to be in several places at once.

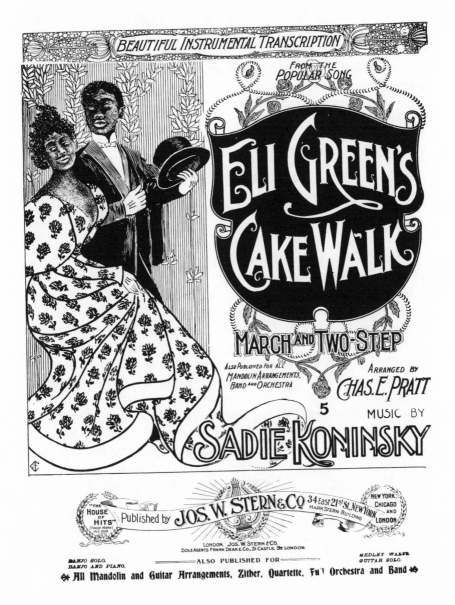

Cakewalks, as published music, actually date back before the 1890s, but they were not syncopated, at least in print, until around 1896. The composers of the music were generally members of the commercial music establishment, and therefore, a number of the cakewalks came out of New York.

The "father of the cakewalk" was Kerry Mills, whose first hit, "Rastus on Parade," in 1895 was followed by a succession of other hits in the genre, including the famous "At a Georgia Camp Meeting," written in 1897. Other noteworthy composers of the cakewalk included J. Bodewalt Lampe, who wrote the delightful "Creole Belles," and Sadie Koninsky, who composed "Eli Green's Cakewalk" in 1896.

It was also in 1896 that ragtime made its official debut on the commercial entertainment scene.

RAGTIME APPEARS

Although probably not the "Orginator of Ragtime," as he billed himself, Ben Harney was the first popular entertainer to play it. In 1896 he introduced ragtime to New York audiences at Tony Pastor's Cafe. Harney, an all-around entertainer, had written a number of good rag songs, including "You've Been a Good Old Wagon" and "Mr. Johnson, Turn Me Loose," but it was his new novelty, ragtime piano, that really caught on. After an astounding success in New York he toured the country with his "discovery." Within weeks after Harney's appearance at Pastor's, ragtime became a fad. Performers (mostly white) were playing, dancing, and singing this new music supposedly in the style of the southern Negroes.

Soon ragtime began to appear in published form. Bert Williams's 1896 number "Oh, I Don't Know, You're Not So Warm," contains an added ragtime piano solo arrangement. But the first completely instrumental rag did not appear until 1897. It was "The Mississippi Rag" by Chicago orchestra director William H. Krell, and it is no accident that it was done by a white orchestra leader, for by the time ragtime came on the scene as published music, it was no longer strictly in the domain of itinerant black musicians but was already a part of the white mainstream "pop"

MARCH A LA RAGTIME.

THE CAKE-WALK IN THE SKY.

WORDS & MUSIC BY

BEN. HARNEY

A RAG-TIME NIGHTMARE.

AUTHOR OF "MR. JOHNSON TURN ME LOOSE" ETC

M. WITMARK & SONS

5

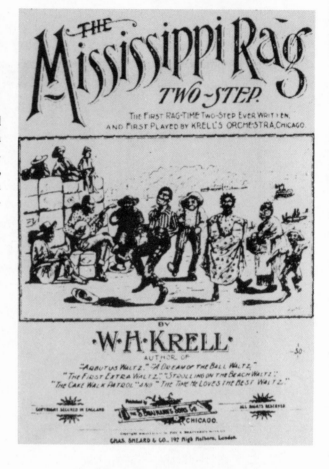

Classical rag published in 1894. Photograph by Charles Klamkin. From *Old Sheet Music*, by Marian Klamkin (New York: Hawthorn, 1975).

culture. Nonetheless, it was always related to blacks in subject matter. The cover illustration of "The Mississippi Rag" pictures a group of "happy darkies" prancing about on the levee to banjo accompaniment among the bales of cotton. This was probably no false stereotype at the time but actually the source of the music. The rag, which is in the form of an orchestral fantasia, is made up of a number of folk themes that most likely did come from the river roustabouts. However, the integration of the separate themes into a cohesive whole was the work of a skillful arranger-composer. This would seem to be the key to the musical superiority of most of the best rags—they are the result of a close association between conventionally trained musicians and the Negro folk sources. In general those composers who were far removed from the folk sources tended to turn out inferior ragtime. Indeed, the

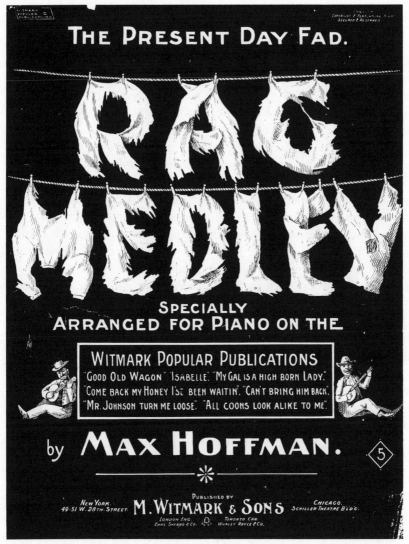

Typical early rag, 1897

myriad of rags that soon flowed from New York's Tin Pan Alley writers demonstrate this point. While often composed by competent arrangers, they lacked what ragtime historian Rudi Blesh has called the racial pungency of the folk rags. Rather, many of them carried the racist stench of the "coon songs," and in fact, a number of the early rags were nothing more than medleys of the current "coon song" favorites in instrumental form. At the same time, the "coon songs" were often being referred to as ragtime songs.

Almost immediately upon its appearance ragtime became an established American institution. Bands performed it at concerts; orchestras played rags for dancing; entertainers sang it; it clanked away on the clumsy mechanical nickelodeons that were located everywhere we now see jukeboxes; and of course, it was played on the pianos of respectable homes and the not-so-respectable "houses" of the tenderloins. However, it was in 1899 that the first ragtime "chart-buster" appeared—Scott Joplin's "Maple Leaf Rag." Although certainly not the first rag—not even Joplin's first rag—in many respects it can be considered to be the most significant rag ever written. It had a unique distinction of being not only an artistic masterpiece but at the same time a phenomenal commercial success. It was the first piece of instrumental music to sell over a million copies. And so it established ragtime as a serious form of music with a wide sales potential. It also established Scott Joplin, a black man, as the virtual king of ragtime composers, a distinction he fully deserved because he remained, throughout his life, the most dedicated champion and serious composer of the idiom.

Joplin and many other black ragtime artists were in a very difficult position at that time. They were part of an increasingly aware, often highly trained, group of serious musicians facing audiences who harbored the conscious or unconscious demand for their music to reflect their own racial prejudices. Joplin himself, though a champion for the respectability and betterment of his race, wrote lyrics in the standard stereotyped imagery of the times. The verse of the otherwise delightful "Ragtime Dance" of 1902 reads:

> I attended a ball last Thursday night
> Given by the "darktown" swells.
> Every coon came out in full dress, alright,
> And the girls were society belles.
>
> The hall was illuminated by electric lights;
> It certainly was a sight to see.
> So many colored folks there without a razor fight,
> T'was a great surprise to me.

Eubie Blake explained the problem:

Back then we could read and write music, but no one wanted to believe that we could. We'd get all the latest music from all the new shows and memorize the parts. People would come in and ask for a tune, say a Victor Herbert song like "The Merry Widow." . . . I'd say, "Anybody ever heard of that?" Then after a bit one of us would say, "I think I've heard that," and he'd lean over and pretend he was singing it for the rest of the fellows, and we'd all play it then. Of course we'd learned it from the music. The customer would say something like, "Oh, those colored boys! Aren't they something; they can't read a note, but they can play naturally so well!"

We used to take our songs into the publishers and smile and talk in dialect and pretend we didn't know anything. They'd always have somebody else doing the arranging. They didn't want to think we could do our own writing.

It's interesting to read the account of one of Eubie's publishers on the same subject:

Not many of those first colored composers read music. They played right out of their heads and an arranger took down the notes as they played. . . . These authentic immigrants from . . . Dixie . . . had a colored rhythm and a colored slant on life, and they hadn't become self-conscious about it either.

We bought so much stuff from colored writers in those days . . . and when every once in a while we viewed the pile of unusable manuscripts which white smiles and mellow voices had cajoled us into buying, we declared a boycott on the whole tribe. . . . When [they] gathered around a piano and harmonized, they could make anything sound good. . . . We got a lot of slaps in our wholesale buying of ragtime numbers, but we also got a lot of pleasure.*

Much of the black music of the times could be characterized as feigning happiness while masking underlying misery. The white music either lacked this type of duality altogether or, in some

---

* Edward B. Marks, *They All Sang* (New York: Viking Press, 1934), pp. 86–87.

cases, faked it. In any case, the majority of the white buyers of ragtime failed to appreciate the profundity of the true ragtime. For them the surface was enough; ragtime was simply "happy colored music." For the black composers it was often much more. As Rudi Blesh sees it:

> It [ragtime] was an idea and that idea was freedom, expressed in a syncopation that danced and shouted over the steady double, oompah beat that—like the old, onerous law and order—sought to restrain it. But sought, now, in vain. The melodies of ragtime were gay, infectious, enchanting, enticing, its harmonies often rich, sometimes haunting. But its intoxicating compulsion came from within the depths of its symbolic drama: the triumph of freedom over slavery.*

This symbolic drama between freedom and slavery could be seen in another light, however. By 1896 the fight for freedom over slavery was years past. The rag composers, such as Scott Joplin and Eubie Blake, might have been the sons of slaves—but they were all born after the Civil War. But the struggle over prejudice and the fight for black identity was becoming increasingly intense. Blacks in America, uprooted from the communal life of the plantation and thrust into often hostile environments in both the South and North, were now fighting the cruelty of loneliness and displacement, which were, in fact, more binding than the chains of slavery that had contained their ancestors. And their music, as an expression of their alienation, was something to which all people caught in the cold, mechanized life of the new industrial age could relate.

It is no accident that many of the best rags can be heard by means of the mechanical piano roll and lose very little. In fact, they often gain depth by the performance. For ragtime, among other things, is an expression of the mechanical age from which it comes. It is machine music, and its haunting quality often arises from the juxtaposition of the older, lively Negro folk tunes within a hollow, metronomic framework. Even when played live, the rags are supposed to be played meticulously, with machinelike preci-

* Rudi Blesh, *Combo: U.S.A.* (Philadelphia, New York, London: Chilton Book Company, 1971), p. 191.

sion. And, like the piano roll, they do not usually end with an upbeat climax, but more often as if someone simply has turned off the power.

Thus, Negro ragtime might be seen in at least four different lights. First, as joyous and creative dance and entertainment music, it reflected the backgrounds of men raised in the black subculture who now had the opportunity to bring their music to the larger public. Second, as parody, it juxtaposed the inane grin of the minstrel-show "coon" against the underlying misery of a suppressed race. Third, as an expression of triumph, it pitted the old law and order against the new freedom from slavery. And finally, as an expression of the loss of innocence, it placed the old manmade folk music in a new, mechanized context.

THE MISSISSIPPI VALLEY, HOME OF RAGTIME

The purest form of ragtime, and what many writers have called the real ragtime, developed in the areas surrounding the Mississippi River, especially around St. Louis. Scott Joplin spent much of his time there, and it was in St. Louis that Tom Turpin's "Harlem Rag," the first published rag actually composed by a Negro, was issued in 1897.

As a city located on the travelways of both the Mississippi River and the railroad lines, St. Louis provided its populace with access to the industrial wonders of the new world, but also, being situated near the somewhat uncivilized West, it retained something of the fresh spirit and optimism of the frontier. Here also many great musical traditions came together. For instance, the European classics were represented by a large German-English community, and a warm Latin flavor was provided by the considerable Spanish-speaking population who had come up the river from Mexico in pursuit of temporary work. But the most important musical influences (to ragtime, at least) were the Negro folk artists—the stevedores of the river and the hundreds of itinerant musicians who constantly moved in and out of town. It was the tenderloin district of St. Louis that provided the clandestine meeting ground for people of these widely varied cultures, races, and social positions. Only there, where society's mores on everything from sex to segregation were totally ignored, could the synthesis

Tom Turpin's "Harlem Rag," 1897. Photograph by Charles Klamkin. From *Old Sheet Music*, by Marian Klamkin (New York: Hawthorn, 1975)

of the social elements that produced ragtime have taken place. The district was wide open for piano players, and its easy life attracted quite a number of them.

It was a fast life with a high "burnout" rate: The sheer exhaustion of constant nocturnal activity took some; others succumbed to the lure of drugs; but perhaps the most horrifying peril these men faced was the then almost incurable disease syphilis, which claimed the lives of many a rag player. Among these last were Scott Joplin and his close friend, Louis Chauvin.

Chauvin's story is particularly tragic. He was reputedly the greatest of all the Mississippi Valley piano players, but he died at the age of twenty-five after having only two strains of his beautiful rags taken down for publishing and posterity. These few measures, which make up the first half of the lovely "Heliotrope

Bouquet" survive only because of Joplin's efforts shortly before Chauvin's death. They provide but a tantalizing glimpse into the soul of a lost genius.

According to most sources, Tom Turpin and his brother, Charlie, were the extremely powerful kingpins of the district, but this fact has been terribly difficult to document. Since they were wealthy individuals, the Turpins seem to have been considered respectable members of the St. Louis community. They were involved in a variety of legitimate business ventures including a number of black theatrical shows, and there is, of course, no reference in any articles of the times to any illicit dealings. Nonetheless, the Turpins' cafe, the Rosebud, was located in the center of the notorious Chestnut Valley red-light district, and there have been many personal references made to their underworld activities.

In the Rosebud, Tom, who weighed over three hundred pounds, had a piano up on blocks so that he could play standing up, and from this vantage point he dominated the musical scene, which included the best of the underground piano players, such as Scott Joplin, whose "Rosebud March" was named after the Turpins' cafe. Turpin himself had six of his robust rags published between 1897 and 1904.

As important as the St. Louis scene was, it was not the only locale in the Mississippi Valley region with the necessary ingredients for the development of folk-inspired ragtime. Sedalia, Missouri (which we will explore later), takes on particular significance because of the activities there of Joplin in the late 1890s.

There were several other cities that produced a number of fine composers, and Kansas City was among them. Charles L. Johnson, probably the foremost composer of the area, published a large number of rags and cakewalks beginning with "Doc Brown's Cakewalk" in 1899 and continuing through "Snookums Rag" in 1918. These works did include a few "dogs," but generally the quality was high. Johnson scored a big hit with "Dill Pickles Rag" and also had several popular songs like "Sweet and Low" that made it to the top of the "charts"; but his best rags are probably the more obscure compositions. "Snookums Rag" is particularly interesting but extremely rare.

Another Kansas City composer, who seems to be rather overlooked, is Euday Bowman. Bowman wrote the famous "12th

"DOC" BROWN.

There is probably no city or town in the country that does not contain a peculiar character— one who is singled out on account of doing certain things that no one else would think of doing, or using strange language that seems senseless, but nevertheless has a meaning which is readily understood when the listener can see the speaker, or other eccentric traits which make these characters a special object for comment.

Of all such that may exist there is probably not one of them that compares with the subject of this sketch for original mirth-provoking characteristics.

"Doc" Brown is noted in Kansas City and vicinity for the many comical and unusual things he does and says but as the "Champion Cake Walker" of the country is where he shines. He has met all comers in this line and has never failed to "take the cake" with one exception, namely, in St. Louis several years ago. The judges at this contest were conceded to be unfair by everyone present, hence this is not considered a defeat.

The rythm commonly called the "Cake Walk" is departed from in this composition purposely with the hope that this style may find as hearty approval as the old.

THE AUTHOR.

Copyrighted 1899. J. W. JENKINS SONS' MUSIC CO.

JUST PUBLISHED! AN INSTANTANEOUS HIT!

"Scandalous Thompson"

By the Author of "DOC" BROWN'S CAKE WALK.

PIANO SOLO, PRICE, 50 Cents. AT ALL MUSIC STORES.

The real "Doc" Brown as he appeared on the back cover of Charles L. Johnson's sheet music for "Doc Brown's Cake Walk." Courtesy of Trebor Tichenor.

Street Rag," which, in its original form, was a complicated "classic" rag. But after being diluted and having its most interesting first strain eliminated, it has become the epitome of the "junk rag"; that is, clichéd, repetitive, and shallow. It was actually one of a series of rags named after streets of Kansas City including the "11th Street Rag," the "13th Street Rag," and "Pettycoat Lane." Bowman also wrote a number of rags in blues forms that feature unorthodox numbers of measures and very tricky bass figures. It is a sad note that this man, who wrote many extremely interesting compositions, is all but unknown today, and his "12th Street Rag," which over the years has made millions for its publisher, was sold outright for fifty dollars.

Kansas City also produced Arthur Pryor, a trombone virtuoso who played with John Philip Sousa. When Sousa discovered that there was a demand for syncopated music, he had Pryor, who was then his assistant director, arrange rags and cakewalks for the band's repertoire. They were extremely successful not only in the United States but also in Paris, where in 1900 the band introduced the cakewalk and ragtime to Europe.

Pryor was called "the Paganini of the trombone," and composed a number of fine rags and cakewalks himself. He was also the director of most of the Sousa band's recording sessions, and later he formed his own band, which in many ways outperformed Sousa's. During his thirty-year career he was responsible for over a thousand different recordings for the Victor label.

Only slightly outside the Mississippi Valley, Nashville, Tennessee, had its own school of ragtime, led by blind composer Charles Hunter. Although a white man, Hunter was close to the Negro folk sources of the music. His rags, with such titles as " 'Possum and 'Taters—A Ragtime Feast" and "Cotton Bolls," are all in a joyful cast and directly reflect the plantation dance music of the fiddle and banjo.

New Orleans, at the southern reaches of the Mississippi Valley, was also affected by the ragtime phenomenon in a number of ways. The newspapers of 1898 show that ragtime concerts and "monster white cakewalks," in which "dancers impersonated the colored population with the use of burnt cork" were being held at least weekly at the respectable West Side Lake Resort. The resort also featured the "Originator of Ragtime," Ben Harney, appearing in concert throughout the year, along with a number of concert bands. One typical band-concert-in-the-park program included:

"Cakewalk in the Sky" .... Ben Harney
"The Darkies' Dream" .... G. L. Lansing
"Mississippi Bubble" .... Chauncey Haines
"Bowery Buck" .... Tom Turpin
"A Ragtime Nightmare" .... Tom Turpin

At the same time, Jack Laine and his friends were "jobbing around" with small five- or six-piece groups playing improvised ragtime.

A caste system in New Orleans separated blacks from "Creoles of color" along a geographical dividing line at Canal Street. Downtown the more educated, musically literate Creoles played in reading bands and orchestras, while uptown the poor, uneducated blacks improvised a simpler yet more potent style of music.

The most popular black reading orchestra was led by John Robichaux. Robichaux made it a point to have the standard orchestrations for any tune the public might request, and these naturally included a variety of rags. It seems most likely that the uptown "hot jazz" bands, like the famous Buddy Bolden's, heard the orchestrations played and adapted parts of them as vehicles for improvisation.

New Orleans, of course, is famous for its Storyville. This almost mythical place is located near the French Quarter and flourished from 1897 to 1917 as the United States' first and, for the next half century, only experiment with "legalized" prostitution. Al Rose, in his excellent book on Storyville, has described the musical environment of the "houses":

> Music in the brothels, though not a necessity, served somewhat the same promotional function as wine and spirits and sex dances and exhibitions in that all helped to get men in a state of readiness for the main event upstairs. From the madam's viewpoint, one supposes, the wine and spirits must have seemed the more valuable stimulant, as compared to music, since she sold the liquor at a profit and made nothing on the music. But at least the music didn't cost her anything, since the musicians were willing to work for tips and it was a

point of pride among many men out for a good time to prove their affluence by tipping them generously. Moreover, lively music undoubtedly put many a customer in a mood to buy another round of drinks, or even another bottle, which would be dispensed to him at inflated prices whose outrageousness presumably bothered him the less the more he drank.

The music varied from brothel to brothel. In many of them a mechanical piano sufficed, with the patrons expected to keep it primed with quarters. In most of the better houses the music was supplied by a live pianist, the "professor," and by a player piano only when the "professor" took a break.*

Perhaps the greatest of these piano-playing professors was Tony Jackson, who has been called by his peers the world's greatest single-handed entertainer. One of the most famous madams of the district, Countess Willie Piazza, recalled, in a 1951 interview, Tony Jackson playing in her establishment:

When things were slow, various pianists, who had worked for us at different times, would drop in after work, and we would enjoy a veritable festival of ragtime. In those days, the stores carried all the latest sheet music; they sent up North for it, to St. Louis, Kansas City, or wherever else it was published. That way, we got to hear the newest numbers.

On such occasions, if Tony Jackson was present, he would literally take over, and there was one customer who could never get his fill of Tony.

He was a minister, and a talented performer in his own right. In fact, I understand that he sometimes played for church dances. But when Sunday rolled around, he was dedicated to denouncing Sin, and once, when he had prepared an especially rousing sermon demanding that Storyville be padlocked, I went to hear him. I sat right up front, across the aisle from his spouse, and when he reached the middle of his oration I lifted my veil, just long enough to wink!**

* Al Rose, *Storyville, New Orleans* (University, Ala.; University of Alabama Press, 1974), p. 103. Reprinted with permission of the author.
** Kay C. Thompson, *Record Changer*, February 1951.

There is little argument that Tony Jackson was the first all-around musician in New Orleans. He had a large following, and most of the piano players of the time, such as Jelly Roll (Ferdinand Joseph La Menthe) Morton and Clarence Williams, freely admitted to being overshadowed and influenced by him. Apparently he could play anything—rags, classics, ballads—and, in addition, he had a marvelous voice. And although almost all of his music was unpublished, he is reported to have been a fine composer of ragtime. In short, he was the complete ragtime entertainer. Al Rose argues, rather convincingly, that it is Tony Jackson who set the pattern as the prototypical ragtime entertainer:

> By now, the world has absorbed, through its various visual communications media, a mental impression of a whorehouse piano player. He is to be seen in the movies and on television, in paintings, illustrations—sometimes in advertisements. Typically, he wears a pearl gray derby, a checkered vest, a stocktie [ascot] with diamond stickpin. His complexion is very dark. He grins readily, flashing rows of brilliant teeth. His piano is an upright, and on the ledge above its keyboard stands an empty whiskey glass and a full bottle. A cigarette dangles from his lower lip.
>
> He wears spats and patent leather shoes—and arm garters, usually bejewelled or otherwise decorated. Virtually every adult now living, at least in the Western world, has been so conditioned to this complex symbol that a fleeting glance at the picture conjures up a host of mental associations.
>
> Every detail of the costume is now a convention and any missing item *is* missed. The television producer will interrupt dress rehearsal to yell, "Somebody forgot his diamond ring! Let's get on the ball!" The public knows exactly how it wants its "professor" to look. It does not ask, "Why can't the vest be striped?" or "Why can't the derby be black or brown?" But if it did, we could safely state, in clear and confident tones, "Because, folks! Because Tony Jackson wore *checkered vests* and *pearl gray* derbies."*

Rose also makes a pretty good analysis of Jackson's motivations in becoming such a formidable performer. In commenting on one

---

* Rose, *Storyville, New Orleans*, p. 109. Reprinted with permission of the author.

old-timer's recollections of Jackson as "happy-go-lucky—not a care in the world!" Rose declares:

> Oh, to be an epileptic, alcoholic, homosexual Negro genius in the Deep South of the United States of America! How could you have a care? Anyone would be happy, naturally, being among the piano virtuosi of his era, permitted to play only in saloons and whorehouses, for pimps and prostitutes and their customers. How could he be anything but "happy-go-lucky"?

Tony Jackson discovered early in life that a young man of such beginnings as his, such "advantages," had to try to please everybody simply to survive. If one played music, one learned to play *every* style, *every* melody. That meant operatic arias, folk songs, coon songs, rags, symphonic strains, novelty tunes, pop tunes, and dirty old blues.

Learn the tunes. Learn the words. Play 'em better, sing 'em better, than anybody alive. "What's the man gonna think, he comes in here slaps a twenty on the box and says, 'Poets and Peasants Overture,' I got to tell him I can't *play* it? Hell, I *learn* all them things, mister! *All* of 'em!"*

Jackson died in 1921 at the age of forty-five, never having recorded or written down any of his rags. Only a few of his songs have survived in published form, most notably the lilting "Pretty Baby." One other composition, "The Naked Dance," survives as played by Jelly Roll Morton, who remembered this number as it was originally played for the naked ladies of the district while they danced for their "high-rolling" customers.**

Undoubtedly Jelly Roll was the second-best piano player–entertainer to come out of the district. And we are fortunate that

---

* Ibid., p. 110. Reprinted with permission of the author.
** Roy Carew, who knew Tony Jackson and Jelly Roll Morton, said that Jackson did not actually compose most of "The Naked Dance." In a letter to the *Ragtime Society Newsletter* in 1966 he said, "He [Tony] used to play a few bars of a 'ratty' strain when he saw me enter the cafe. I played as much as I could for Jelly Roll, and asked him if he remembered a tune like that. He said he did, and proceeded to compose a number based on a few bars. So it was Jelly Roll that composed the number for me, similar, but not the same as Tony played."

he recorded quite extensively from the early 1920s up to the time of his death in 1941.

Jelly's life was extremely complicated and controversial. He was, like Tony Jackson, a complete singing, joke-telling, piano-playing entertainer, but he was also a key figure in the development of jazz music. During his career he traveled all across the country doing everything from playing vaudeville shows to pimping.* He made a large number of records both as a soloist and as the leader of several fine New Orleans–style ensemble groups, and he composed a sizable volume of rags, stomps, tangos, and blues. There is really so much to his output and so many ways in which the material can be evaluated that I hesitate to do so here. I would refer the reader to Alan Lomax's book *Mister Jelly Roll* and to a magnificent set of records that Jelly made in 1938 for the Library of Congress (see Discography). The series documents the life and music of Jelly Roll Morton and his many associates.

On one of these records Jelly superbly demonstrated the way the "Maple Leaf Rag" was played in St. Louis, and the way he transformed it into his own arrangement. And on another he demonstrated how he assembled the famous "Tiger Rag" from schottisches, quadrilles, and minuets that were played for the upper-class dances. And throughout, Jelly related his stories in a matter-of-fact, straightforward manner with full explanations of his musical theories:

> Ragtime is a certain type of syncopation and only certain tunes can be played in that idea. But jazz is a style that can be applied to any type of tune. . . . If you can't manage to put tinges of Spanish in your tunes, you will never be able to get the right seasoning, I call it, for jazz. . . .
>
> Regardless to any tempo you might set, especially if it was meant for a dance tune, you ought to end up at that same tempo. . . .
>
> . . . the medium slow tunes did more for the development of jazz . . . due to the fact that you could always hit a note twice . . . when ordinarily you would hit it once, which gave the music a very good flavor. . . .

* *The Autobiography of Pops Foster, New Orleans Jazzman* (Berkeley/Los Angeles: University of California Press, 1971), p. 33.

Always have a melody going some kind of way against a background of perfect harmony with plenty of riffs—meaning figures. . . . No jazz piano player can really play good jazz unless they try to give an imitation of a band. . . .

If a tune haven't got a break in it, it's always necessary to arrange some kind of a spot to make a break. A break . . . is a musical surprise.

Jazz music is to be played sweet, soft, plenty rhythm. . . .

You can't make crescendos and diminuendos when one is playing triple forte. . . . You got to be able to come down in order to go up. . . .*

In Jelly's playing you can hear the propulsive rhythmic concepts that were the hallmark of New Orleans traditional jazz. This is the synthesis of all the New Orleans music sources by an intelligent, highly original artist who was fully capable of transferring his ideas to paper or realizing them in a recording studio.

THE TURN OF THE CENTURY

After the first few years of the new century it would become increasingly difficult to isolate ragtime geographically, but there were clearly several schools: The itinerant musicians of the South were still playing folk music, but this was a dying trend—most ragtime was losing contact with its roots; Scott Joplin, who had given the movement its big boost, would, in the next few years, put more of his effort into making ragtime a composer's art form; in New Orleans Jelly Roll Morton and Tony Jackson played rags with the forward-moving, improvisatory feel of jazz; in New York the mass-media brains sold ragtime as the mainstay of popular music while on other parts of the East Coast a whole group of two-fisted black piano players were composing rags that would be the basis of the later Harlem stride school (see Chapter 6). Meanwhile, every large and small city had some ragtime activity, and composers and musicians of all types were entering the field.

* From the Jelly Roll Morton Library of Congress recordings, as transcribed in Alan Lomax, *Mister Jelly Roll* (New York: Grossett and Dunlap, 1950), pp. 62–66.

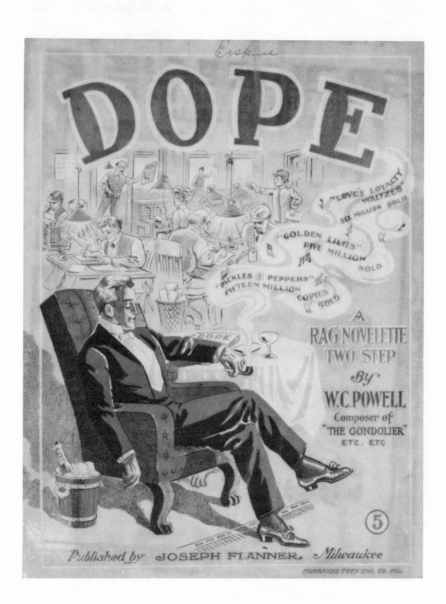

The amazing popularity of this music was not without its detractors, however. Brun Campbell, one of Joplin's pupils, who roamed the Midwest at the turn of the century, recalled:

At the beginning of written ragtime in 1897, ragtime was socially and musically in the "dog house"; or, more specifically, in the bawdy house (for that is where it was first heard and got its start), and in other places like the old barrel houses and the cheap dives of the red-light districts. Because ragtime was revolutionary, it was not respectable, either among the whites or Negroes of the upper and middle classes—not because it was a Negro music, but because it was underworld music. At that time the underworld was powerful, and was the symbol of sin. Every city of over five thousand population has its well-defined red-light district. Right from the beginning, preachers preached that ragtime was the music of the devil, and it was under fire by most of the churches and Women's Temperance Clubs of America.*

The American Federation of Musicians summed up the attitude of the legitimate musical establishment at their annual meeting in Denver, Colorado, in 1901; in their official statement they labeled ragtime "musical rot" and pledged to discourage its playing and publication.

It remained for such great composers as Scott Joplin to posthumously vindicate ragtime in the eyes of the music world at large.

* Brun Campbell, *Rag Times* (November 1970): 3.

3

The Classic Rag

"Ragging" Good Music

BY EDWARD BAXTER PERRY

It is no uncommon thing in these days of rampant frivolity and seemingly almost universal imbecility to hear in hotels and other places of public gathering not only a continuous series of the trashiest ragtime pieces played on a mechanical piano, or even by a so-called orchestra, which are a deliberate insult to all intelligent persons present, but even well-known good compositions by recognized composers of high standing perverted and distorted out of all semblance to the original works and vulgarized beyond the power of language to express by being changed and twisted into cheap ragtime rhythms.

Ragtime is syncopation gone mad, and its victims, in my opinion, can only be treated successfully like the dog with rabies, namely, with a dose of lead. Whether it is simply a passing phase of our decadent art culture or an infectious disease which has come to stay, like la grippe and leprosy, time alone can show. . . .

Although the above quote appeared in *Etude* magazine in 1918, it was typical of the many attacks from the musical establishment aimed at ragtime throughout its popularity. In spite of such epithets there was a concerted effort to make ragtime respectable. To this end Scott Joplin and his white publisher, John Stark, coined the term *classic rag* to denote the very finest of the instrumental rags. Joplin was the first creator of the genre so defined, and unquestionably he alone provided the creative momentum that raised ragtime out of the category of entertainment and made it a composer's art form.

SCOTT JOPLIN: THE KING OF RAGTIME COMPOSERS

It is axiomatic that creative geniuses are seldom recognized in their own time (at least fifty years are generally required for full appraisal), and Joplin was no exception. He lived completely within the tradition of the true "suffering artist," producing a continuous flow of revolutionary musical thought that stemmed from deep frustration.

Joplin was first of all black, and he grew up in a paradoxical period of the late nineteenth century when black men were making great strides toward equality but simultaneously experiencing increased repression from white society. In addition, Joplin was the victim of a number of tragic personal circumstances that culminated in his complete insanity and death at the age of forty-nine.

He was born on November 24, 1868, near Marshall, Texas, and spent most of his youth in Texarkana, a city divided between Arkansas and Texas, with the black population living on the Arkansas side. Joplin's parents, newly freed slaves, were both musically inclined, as were all of their six children. Giles Joplin, Scott's father, had been a plantation violinist; his mother, Florence, played the banjo and sang. From his father Scott learned the waltzes, schottisches, and polkas that Giles had played for his white "employers" along with the syncopation that had been common on the plantation. But Scott probably picked up most of his musical education from his mother.

As a result of an early separation, Florence Joplin was left with the task of raising the six children alone. This she did by doing domestic work in the white folks' houses and by taking in laundry. Through her influence Scott was exposed to the Negro folk music of the local church. He demonstrated his remarkable musical ability as a small child by playing and improvising on numbers he had heard in church. And although his musical talent had been discouraged by his father, his mother supported it by taking Scott to the "big houses" that she worked in and allowing him to play the pianos there. Later she managed to scrape together the money to purchase a piano for him to use at home.

While still a youngster Joplin began actively to pursue a musical career. His talent attracted the attention of several local music teachers, who acquainted him with the classical music literature of the day, and it wasn't long before he was playing at various church functions and socials. But Joplin was also exploring the secular music of the Texarkana area. He visited and began playing at the various honky-tonks, clubs, and eating places where the "low down" transient musicians were entertaining. And it wasn't long before Joplin was joining them.

While still a teen-ager he organized the Texas Medley Quartet, which toured the Texas-Arkansas-Missouri area. By 1885, at the age of seventeen, he was singing, playing piano, mandolin, and guitar; and he had shifted his home base to St. Louis, where he worked at the Silver Dollar Saloon for "Honest John" Turpin, the father of Tom and Charlie Turpin.

For the next eight years Joplin built up his reputation as a performer all around the Midwest; then in 1893 he joined the hundreds of other itinerant musicians who congregated in Chicago for the World's Columbian Exposition. Although not involved in the fair proper, these traveling troubadours provided entertainment on the outskirts of the fairgrounds. It is reported that Joplin had a small band assembled for the event, consisting of cornet (which he played), clarinet, tuba, and baritone horn.

There is very little documentation as to exactly what Joplin did at the fair, but it is my impression that the experience must have been a real eye-opener to him in many ways. The fair featured, from time to time, several black concert artists, such as Madame Sissieretta Jones (the operatic vocalist who was known as Black Patti); violinist Joseph Douglas (who performed on "Colored American Day," one of the special features of the fair); and also, probably for the first time, there were assembled a number of black composers and artists who were and would continue to be working at the task of bringing American Negro folk music into the realm of legitimacy.

The fair had many messages: For one thing, it signaled the opening of a whole new world of technological advancement—a

Cover for 1901 edition of "Maple Leaf Rag." Photograph by Charles Klamkin. From *Old Sheet Music*, by Marian Klamkin (New York: Hawthorn, 1975).

world of staggering potential. Secondly, it seemed to promise a piece of the action to blacks. Joplin returned from the fair with enough encouragement to work seriously toward publication of his music, and in 1895 he began doing just that.

Joplin's first published numbers were rather maudlin affairs in the genteel tradition, but during this time he was gaining experience and building a reputation both as a composer and performer. Finally he settled in Sedalia, Missouri, and it was here that he began his career as a composer of ragtime.

Sedalia, which was an end point for many cattle drives, was a thriving frontier town, and it held many attractions for Joplin. First, the Smith College for Negroes, which provided him with the opportunity to expand and refine his serious study of music, was located there. On the other hand, the city also had a large red-light district, which could provide work and contact with the underground world of Negro folk music. Sedalia also had several music publishers.

It would seem that Joplin actually had some of his rags in manuscript form as early as 1897 but was not able to sell them to a publisher until the ragtime vogue was in full swing. His "Maple Leaf Rag" was turned down in 1899 by Perry and Sons, of Sedalia, and also by Carl Hoffman, of Kansas City, who instead published his "Original Rags." But in the same year Joplin finally met John Stark, owner of a small music store in Sedalia, who did publish the "Maple Leaf Rag" and went on to become the lifelong champion of classic ragtime.

There are at least three different versions of how Stark happened to decide to publish Joplin's masterpiece. According to John Stark's son, Will, who did arrangements for Stark and was himself a ragtime composer, Joplin came into the store with a small boy, sat down at the piano, and played the "Maple Leaf Rag" while the youngster stepped it off. From Will's account, John Stark actually did not want to publish it, but Will was so taken by the lad's dance that they decided to buy it anyway.*

According to another version of the story, Joplin's lawyer called the attention of Stark to the music, and a third version sets the first Joplin-Stark meeting in the Maple Leaf Club, where Joplin played piano.

There are also varying descriptions of the Maple Leaf Club. By one account we get a picture of a social center of sorts with a fairly large room where various political meetings were held and where Joplin rehearsed with the Queen City Concert Band, in which he played second cornet. Other accounts portray the club as primarily a saloon where the piano players played for tips and the whores picked up their clientele. Most likely the club had at least two rooms and was certainly large enough to handle all of these various activities.

In any case, Stark was genuinely moved by the music and made what was at the time an unusual contract with Joplin: It allowed Joplin not only a flat fee of fifty dollars for the rag but also pro-

* Dorothy Brockhoff, "Missouri Was the Birth Place of Ragtime," *St. Louis Post-Dispatch*, January 1961.

THE MAPLE LEAF CLUB.

SEDALIA,

121 EAST MAIN ST.
W. J. WILLIAMS, PROP.

MO.

—THE GOOD TIME BOYS.—

WILLIAM'S PLACE, for Williams, E. Cook
Allie Ellis, Taylor Williams. Will give a
good time, for instance Master Scott Joplin, the entertainer. W. J. Williams the
slow wonder said that H. L. Dixon, the
cracker-jack around ladies said E. Cook,
the ladies masher told Dan Smith, the
clever boy, he saw L n Williams, the
dude, and he said that there are others but not so good.
These are the members of the "Maple Leaf Club,".
Don't forget Jake Powel, the plunger and King of
kitchen machanic.

Front and back of business card for the original Maple Leaf Club.
Courtesy of Larry Melton.

vided royalties on a continuing basis. Unfortunately, neither man
foresaw the importance of procuring any musical rights other
than publishing; neither Joplin nor Stark, therefore, ever saw any
money from the mechanical rights for the rag. These included
those for the popular player-piano rolls and phonograph records,
which would soon assume a great importance on the commercial
scene. Furthermore, Stark and Joplin made only one and one-half
cents apiece for each piece of sheet music sold.

Stark, who might well be described as a romantic pragmatist, probably typified the somewhat naïve values of the United States "frontier" mentality. He was born in 1841, fought the good fight in the Civil War (on the Blue side), and then made his living with a Conestoga wagon as a frontier salesman, first of ice cream, and then organs. He does not appear to have been ruthless enough to be a great businessman, but with the "Maple Leaf Rag" he stumbled onto a good thing indeed. In spite of its difficulty, the sales of the piece were fantastic at the time—75,000 copies in the first year. The music sold as fast as Stark could keep it in print.

The next rag to be published by Stark was "The Swipesy Cakewalk," a collaboration by Joplin and one of his young pupils, Arthur Marshall.

It has been believed for years that in Joplin's early collaborations with Marshall and Scott Hayden, his other student, that one composer would do one or two strains and the other would complete the piece. It would appear, however, that in most cases the works were joint efforts from top to bottom. Joplin worked together with his pupils for hours on end in constructing these rags. There is even a possibility that Arthur Marshall helped with the composition of the "Maple Leaf Rag." Nevertheless, it was Joplin's inspiration that produced the music. As Marshall once said years later, "Ragtime was already around Sedalia, but Joplin got things going!"*

Within a year after his initial success with the "Maple Leaf Rag," Joplin was already pushing for an expanded form of ragtime. He rented Woods Opera House in Sedalia and staged "The Ragtime Dance," and apparently it was very well received. It was an extremely advanced composition for the time in that Joplin was attempting to integrate music, words, and dance in one work. This was common to the Afro-American musical tradition, but here was Joplin attempting to codify that tradition in European musical terms. Probably owing to the long and complicated nature of the work, it would seem to have had little commercial potential as sheet music. With reluctance Stark published it in 1902, and just as he had expected, despite its stage success, this ambitious effort

* Interview: Mildred Marshall Steward, daughter of Arthur Marshall.

was a smash flop. Two years later Stark issued the work in shortened form as a rag without verse, words, or dance directions.

Around 1900 Stark moved his operation to St. Louis, and Joplin, who was then at the height of his national popularity, soon followed. The next few years saw him in demand as a performer, and his rags sold well. By the end of 1902 Stark had published "Peacherine Rag," "The Easy Winners," and "Elite Syncopations," as well as the delightful "The Entertainer." But Joplin was still not satisfied; he continued to work for classical status of his music, and he composed a ragtime opera called *A Guest of Honor*. The work was copyrighted in 1903 and supposedly performed by the Joplin Ragtime Opera Company, but it was never published, and at present, despite rumors to the contrary, there are no known copies in existence.

While in Sedalia, Joplin had married Belle Hayden, the sister-in-law of Scott Hayden. But the marriage never worked and was dissolved in 1905. Contributing factors to the union's demise seem to have been the loss of a child and Belle's inability or unwillingness to adapt to Joplin's musical career; a complicated love life may also have played a part. (Charles Thompson, a St. Louis piano player, recalled one of Joplin's pieces, "Leola," which he said was written in 1904 for a girl Joplin was in love with.) In any case, by 1906 Joplin hit one of his nadirs of depression, and his compositional output nearly dried up.

By 1907 Joplin seems to have "bottomed out" and gotten himself sufficiently back together to start a new life. He settled in New York, where John Stark already had set up an office, and there he met and married Lottie Stokes, who, unlike Belle, was sympathetic to Joplin's ambitions. She provided a comfortable atmosphere and moral support for his musical activities throughout the rest of his life; for years after his death the Joplin house was still a meeting place for jazz and ragtime musicians in New York.

But even in this supportive domestic environment Joplin became increasingly tormented by his personal devils. The years 1907 to 1909 saw the publication of around fifteen more works of brilliant composition, but there is some doubt as to whether or not he could even play them. By that time syphilis was already taking hold, and by the time he was forty, his health was rapidly deteriorating. Eubie Blake recalls Joplin at this stage:

They gave me an introduction to Scott—and—I talked to him about half an hour and I have never seen him since. You heard this tune "We Want Cantor, We Want Cantor." When I first heard that tune it was in nineteen—either seven, eight, or nine, in Washington. "We want Joplin. We want Joplin!"—and he kept saying, "Fellas, I don't play." He could hardly talk—he was sick—his health was gone, he was very ill. Hughie Wolford was sharp—Jimmie Meredith, sharp piano player. Philadelphia Jack "The Bear." These are piano players.—Sammy Ewell, the guy that played five-finger bass—five fingers! I've seen him do that! And Scott knew he couldn't compare with these fellas. So, they kept after him, and he went to the piano, and played. It was pitiful. I almost cried—and the guys, especially Hughie, you know, made a face at his playin'. They didn't think—that if it wasn't for him, that music would have been wiped out. Like I always tell people when I'm on the stage, "He had the *nerve* to put it down on paper."

Joplin's folk opera *Treemonisha* became his consuming passion and frustration from 1907 until his death. These last years were spent in a vain attempt to get the opera backed financially and performed. Stark, wisely from his point of view, refused to publish the work. Because of this and Stark's desire, now, to buy Joplin's rags outright with no royalty agreement, the two men split in 1909. Joplin retired more and more from performance into composition. By 1910 his published output had narrowed to a trickle: "Stoptime Rag" was published in 1910; the opera *Treemonisha* was published in 1911 by Joplin himself; "Scott Joplin's New Rag" appeared in 1912; and finally in 1914 the haunting "Magnetic Rag" was copyrighted by the Scott Joplin Music Company.

Joplin's consuming obsession was never brought to fruition. In 1915 he managed to organize a meager performance of *Treemonisha* without orchestra or costumes, and the production was poorly received by a black Harlem audience. This final setback put him over the hill. His periods of lucidity became ever more rare, and in 1916 Lottie was forced to have him committed to the Manhattan State Hospital on Ward's Island.

Earlier that same year Joplin had recorded several hand-played piano rolls. All of them seem to have been corrected for mistakes with one exception: a roll of the "Maple Leaf Rag" made for the Uni-Record piano-roll company. This roll provides a sad yet fascinating insight into Joplin's tortured mind a few months before the final breakdown. The playing is irregular and jerky and full of strange mistakes. The performance gives the horrible impression that the whole thing is somehow going to break down completely before the end.

When Joplin died on April 1, 1917, he left behind a number of unpublished scores, many of which Rudi Blesh saw in the 1940s when he was doing research for *They All Played Ragtime*. Tragically, at Lottie Joplin's death all of those scores disappeared and are presumed to have been discarded. Included were orchestrations for several rags, such as "Pretty Pansy" and "Recitative Rag," and the full orchestration for *Treemonisha*.

THE CLASSIC RAG

There is no clear indication as to when Joplin actually began to think of his music as classical, but we can assume from his activities that he was contemplating that possibility at least as early as 1900, although the term *classic* was not applied to ragtime until some time later when it became associated with the John Stark catalogue of rags. During his twenty or so years of activity in the business Stark published the instrumental rags of a number of composers that he labeled classic. The following is a typical Stark advertisement:

Don't confound these numbers with the coon songs, or imitations by the *commercial* composer. They stand out unique and alone, towering over the mess of rag trash on the market like Pikes Peak over a mole-hill. It is a sign of ability and culture to play them, and they are welcomed in the drawing-rooms and boudoirs of good taste. Have you looked for their finish along with the season's hits? Nay, they have *come to stay*. Rivals arise each season, but these classics put them to sleep in one, two, three order. Play these numbers. Not too fast. Not carelessly. In their matchless measures is a sentimental *CONTENT* that only the player who is also a *MUSICIAN* can reveal.

STARK MUSIC CO.

Although it could be said that many of the rags in the Stark catalogue didn't come up to the high standards set by Joplin's works, the idea seemed to be this: To write classic rags was to write *not* for the commercial public, then, but for the ages—to achieve some kind of universal perfection. And though drawing on folk sources for inspiration, it is art music written for its own sake, primarily as an expression of the artist-composer. There are many arguments as to which rags are classic and which are not, but it would seem that to the extent that the primary motivation of the author was to write this sort of "art" music, the rag could be called classic. Further, virtually all of the classic-rag composers were inspired directly or indirectly by Scott Joplin.

Studying the period in which the classic rag flourished, it is possible to discern shifts in content and form as the composers of the new genre, led by Joplin, explored its possibilities. And although for this reason it is impossible to find definitive characteristics that distinguish classic rags from the other instrumental rags of the period, we can isolate certain generally common factors.

When it first appeared, the instrumental rag was thought of as a collection of folk tunes tied together to form a longer work. Joplin's first published rag, "Original Rags" illustrates the point. Its title page reads: "Original Rags picked by Scott Joplin, and arranged by Charles N. Danials." The word *picked* is misleading, but it does indicate a series of short pieces, all originally composed by Scott Joplin. "Original Rags" is a good, cohesive work but lacks the unity of Joplin's next published piece, "Maple Leaf Rag."

The "Maple Leaf Rag" would have to be thought of as a single piece of music, and its format can be considered prototypical of the classic rag. It contains four sixteen-bar themes in the form: *a-a-b-b-a-c-c-d-d*. (The initial theme, *a*, is repeated once more after the second theme, *b*, and the key signature changes to the sub-

dominant at the *trio*, section *c*.) But this is by no means the definitive form.

In looking at the works of Joplin, it is possible to see constant
deviation from any formal pattern. Even the number of measures
in a theme was expanded to twenty-four, rather than the usual
sixteen, in one of his rags. In fact, looking at Joplin's total output
of piano works, around fifty-five in all, there are at least twenty-
four different forms. And a similar variety of structures can be
found in the works of other major rag composers. The key factor is
that these musicians *were not* concerned so much with form as
with artistic expression. This makes it somewhat difficult to get at
the essence of ragtime—but Joplin has given us some clues.

In the introduction to his *School of Ragtime*, published in 1908,
Joplin stated that the object of the work was to "assist amateur
players in giving the 'Joplin Rags' that *weird* and intoxicating
effect intended by the composer" [italics mine]. This quality of
"weirdness" seems to be at the heart of classic ragtime, and it
permeates the rags on many levels: structurally, melodically,
harmonically, rhythmically. It is this illusive factor that gives ragtime both its complicated intellectual content and its great emotional depth. And this can first be seen in the overall mood of the
music. There is a surface gaiety juxtaposed against an underlying
rigidity and sadness. If it were not for this tension in the music,
the mood would be light and one-dimensional. Good ragtime
might be humorous, but it is rarely happy. This is the same difference that distinguishes Charlie Chaplin from countless anony-
mous slapstick clowns.

The most obvious method of building in this tension is by the
use of *rhythmic* clashes of syncopation. The conformity of the left
hand, with its rigid "boom-chick" pattern (alternating in duple
time a low bass note with a chord), against the rhythmic independence of the right hand is the basic rhythmic structure of
ragtime. But this is only a starting point for building rhythmic
tension. The rags also stop and start irregularly; a great flurry of
notes will be followed, perhaps, by a surprisingly simple, unsyn-
copated phrase. The listener is kept constantly off balance.

Despite the fact that most of the rags are built on the standard
tonic/dominant/subdominant chord structure that was prevalent
in march music and in the Negro folk music of the nineteenth
century, there were a number of idiosyncrasies in many of them

Joplin's "Fig Leaf Rag." Photograph by Charles Klamkin. From *Old Sheet Music*, by Marian Klamkin (New York: Hawthorn, 1975).

that gave them a sometimes "weird" harmonic structure. There are several probable reasons for this that are related to the Afro-American roots of the music.[*] First there is the tendency to ambivalence to the third, fourth, and seventh (and sometimes fifth) notes of the European scale. This is brought about by the differences between the African five-note scale, which is based on pure harmonics that occur in nature, and the European seven-note scale which is tempered to facilitate changes of key. The most noticeable difference in concept is in the third in a chord, which is the interval that determines whether it sounds major or minor to

[*] Ann Charters, "Negro Folk Elements in Classic Ragtime," *Ethnomusicology*, 5, no. 3 (September 1961): 174–183.

our ears. (A chord with a raised third is major and sounds basically bright or happy to us. A lowered third becomes minor and sounds sad.) Both are a compromise to the pure third—major is slightly higher and minor considerably lower. The African only hears the pure third which is actually what we talk about in jazz as the blue note.

In ragtime the basic ambivalence of Afro-American music toward this third is brought out in other ways—the third is avoided as much as possible, the major and minor third are played together or close together, or the whole major/minor feel is rapidly alternated. As an example, the opening bars of the last strain of Joplin's "The Entertainer" could be considered either major or minor.

A second harmonic characteristic is the constant shifting between full harmony and single-note or two-note passages. This practice, like that of using rhythmic displacements, provides a constant succession of surprises.

The classic rag composers were also fond of introducing unexpected changes of key and complicated chord changes into their music. To fully appreciate this, we can contrast it to more contemporary music. In mainstream jazz and popular music the recent thrust has often been toward a "softening" of the chords. This means that the tonic chord (for example, C major, which contains the notes C, E, and G) might be played as a major sixth (C6: C, E, G, and A); similarly, a seventh chord (such as C7: C, E, G, B♭) might be played as a ninth (with a D) or thirteenth (with an A). The result is that many of the notes in the chords are duplicated in succeeding chords. For example, in changing from a tonic C major chord (C, E, G) to the subdominant F major chord (F, A, C) only one note is the same in each triad (the C); but if the sixth, or A, is added to the C chord, there is a duplication of two notes in the chords, both C and A. The chord change then sounds less violent to the ear. In most ragtime, however, the chords are kept fairly pure, and the changes thus produced are more dramatic. There is also a tendency to place unusual emphasis on diminished (for example, C diminished: C, E♭, G♭, A) and other chords that would ordinarily be mere "passing chords."

So, here is a whole range of musical tools employed by the ragtimers to produce great musical and emotional tension. And whether it is resolved in jubilance, as in the "Maple Leaf Rag," say, or in some other dramatic manner, the net result leaves the listener somehow swept up and indeed intoxicated by the sounds. This is musical energy arising not from high speed or dexterity in performance but from solid internal factors carefully woven into the musical structure.

JOPLIN'S RAGS

Of all the ragtime music, Joplin's is the most purely artistic and autobiographical. It is music written for its own sake and always reflective of Joplin's personal life, both in title and conception. Trebor Tichenor has divided Joplin's life and works into three periods, which he defines as follows:

1. The early period, characterized by simple, flowing melodic lines of great beauty and much folk inspiration, such as "Weeping Willow," "Easy Winners," and "The Entertainer";
2. The peak period, which starts about 1904 with "Cascades," when his rags begin to strut; his conceptions are more expansive and there is a new grandiose quality; "Fig Leaf" is a masterpiece of this period; and
3. The experimental period, characterized by rags with bolder harmonies and more elements of romantic classical music; "Euphonic Sounds" and his opera *Treemonisha* are in line with the third period, and the few rags of this period may be off-shoots from his work on the opera. *

* Arnold S. Caplin, *Scott Joplin Ragtime*, Vol. 2 (Canaan, N.Y.: Biograph Records, 1971), BLP-1008Q. From the liner notes.

I personally find it difficult to make such precise distinctions. There is certainly a clear connection to the folk sources in the early rags and a leaning toward the experimental in the later ones, especially "Magnetic Rag," but all the ones in between are extremely difficult to categorize. "Paragon Rag" from 1909 sounds a great deal like "Weeping Willow" from 1903. And the *trio* of "Eugenia" from 1905 seems in many ways as "experimental" as "Scott Joplin's New Rag" of 1912.

One problem, which Joplin's biographer, Addison Reed, has pointed out in analysis of these rags is that since no manuscripts now exist, we don't know when the music was actually written—we only know when it was published.* In many cases the publishing date bears little relation to the actual date of composition. This gives the academic musicologists fits because they can't accurately chart Joplin's "compositional progress."

Further complicating the evaluation in some minds is Joplin's unstable mental condition. Obviously a man who lost his marbles toward the end of his career couldn't have been making steady progress. As jazz historian Martin Williams put it:

> Joplin's "last period" is a strange collection of contradictions. Some of his rags reach more toward concert music than did any Jazz up to Lennie Tristano's, while others seem to revert to his 1900 style. Profoundly ambitious passages lie side by side with meaningless, mechanical ditties. It is not hard to find in these compositions a reflection of approaching derangement—he lost his mind in 1916.**

I believe many musicologists fail to look at the nature of the creative process. Joplin's flight into experimentation would surely have occurred in relation to his personal needs and frustrations. The "weird quotient" goes up with the personal need for such expression. A period of experimentation could naturally have occurred in 1905 around the time of his divorce and again when

* Addison W. Reed, *The Life and Works of Scott Joplin* (Ph.D. diss., University of North Carolina, 1973), p. 53.
** Martin Williams, *The Art of Jazz* (New York: Oxford University Press, 1959), p. 16.

hardships mounted in later years. In between, a certain amount of simple joy might have crept in—not meaningless, but *simple*.

To see Joplin's late rags as a "strange collection of contradictions" also misses the point. Again, *simplicity is not necessarily meaningless*. "Magnetic Rag" does indeed include parts reminiscent of Joplin's 1900 style, but they serve to set up the "profound" parts. Here is a terrifying mixture of the familiar and the agonizing unknown. It is in fact *more* profound for being able to bring these opposites into focus. The music is heavy with the weight of Joplin's approaching schizoid nightmare—but that is not a weakness.

TREEMONISHA

As William Schafer and Johannes Riedel have pointed out in their book, *The Art of Ragtime*, "It [*Treemonisha*] is not . . . an 'opera' in any conventional sense; instead it is something much more interesting: *it is what Joplin conceived an opera as being*."*

This was Joplin's greatest attempt to synthesize all of his musical and ideological thought. It contains elements of ragtime, yet *Treemonisha* is not pure ragtime; it is actually a folk opera and harks back to the original folk sources of ragtime from which Joplin drew his lifelong inspiration.

Such an undertaking was doomed to failure—but failure on such a grand scale that it cannot be dismissed lightly. It is a magnificent attempt, and parts of it approach greatness. Sadly, it was constructed against terrific odds; Joplin had neither the health nor the opportunity to perfect the form, and the public would give him little support. Again, to quote Schafer and Riedel:

> A social and historical principle seems to dictate that cultures losing track of their real needs and desires get precisely what they deserve. It is not surprising that America was not prepared to listen to *Treemonisha* in 1911. After decades of unparalleled crassness, vulgarity, and social retrogression—the "Gilded Age" and collapse of Radical Reconstruction in the

* William J. Schafer and Johannes Riedel, *The Art of Ragtime* (Baton Rouge, La.: Louisiana State University Press, 1973), p. 218.

late nineteenth century—America was hardly prepared for a naïve, delicate and almost translucently gentle operatic style. It was not interested in black social or aesthetic advances, and it had no curiosity about Scott Joplin, once his phenomenal success with "Maple Leaf Rag" faded from the popular mind.*

Treemonisha is actually like the classic rag taken one step further. A classic rag is a combination of Negro folk-music sources in the framework of a European march—*Treemonisha* is also a combination of these folk inspirations, but in the grander framework of a European opera. However, though Joplin sought the status of the opera, it was on his own terms. He was not a black man trying to write an opera like the great (white) European composers—he was a black man, or rather he was *Scott Joplin*, creating a piece of art from all of his own experiences, which included opera. As such, *Treemonisha*, like ragtime music itself, was an entirely new art form that was probably only approached in style in the 1920s by the Kurt Weill and Bertolt Brecht collaborations, such as *The Threepenny Opera*.

The music itself is the strongest part of *Treemonisha*. Much of it might be termed overdramatic; there are a number of lengthy, ominous-sounding diminished-chord runs that seem to betray Joplin's unrefined frustration—but there is still a great deal of musical worth. The finale, "Doin' the Real Slow Drag," especially ranks with the best of anything Joplin ever wrote.

Where *Treemonisha* fails is in the libretto. In it Joplin presented the crux of his fixation and frustration: He saw education as the one great hope for the betterment of his race. It was already quite apparent, even in his time, that education for blacks was not the panacea for racial prejudice, but Joplin had built his whole career, as well as the opera, on that assumption. The educated heroine, Treemonisha, leads her brethren down the path of enlightenment away from the ways of superstition and ignorance. They have but to accept the high road of education and all will be right.

Whether this view is realistic and accurate or naïve and simplistic, the work still has to be seen as a straightforward statement

* Ibid., pp. 224–225.

of sincere belief. It is pure Joplin who, although the product of a time in which sycophantic worship of European art was the rule, nevertheless expressed himself as a black American and a creative genius. *Treemonisha* may not have been his finest work by classical-music standards, but by any historical account it is a heroic effort.

OTHER CLASSIC RAG COMPOSERS

Although Scott Joplin was the guiding influence behind the classic ragtime scene, he was by no means the only composer of the genre. There were many others, most of whom knew Joplin directly and were published by John Stark.

Joplin's most direct influence was over his two young pupils and friends from the pre-1900 Sedalia days, Scott Hayden and Arthur Marshall. Hayden died in 1915 having published only four compositions—all collaborations with Joplin. (Bob Darch later discovered a rag called "Pear Blossoms," a partially completed manuscript by Hayden. This he himself completed and published in the second edition of *They All Played Ragtime*.)

But in the case of Marshall we are more fortunate. Marshall not only collaborated with Joplin on the delightful "Swipesy Cakewalk" but also wrote a number of his own rags that reveal his individual style as being quite separate from Joplin's.

Marshall, like Joplin, was a constant traveler in the early years. He moved about in the Mississippi Valley region and up to Chicago, often traveling with minstrel shows and playing the honkytonks all around the area. His rags are alive with the earthiness of these folkways and contain a great amount of idiomatic coloration. Marshall, more than any other composer, carefully notated the ornaments that seem to have been common to many of the folk-rag players. Particularly interesting in this regard is his 1908 composition "Ham and ! in Ragtime," which Trebor Tichenor in the January 1966 issue of *The Ragtime Review* called "a rare jewel of great ragtime, a classic rag of wonderful, explicit, footstomping character with some funky jazz features that make it stand alone." And pianist Bob Wright in the same article has stated that "it contains elements of phrasing and emotional quali-

ties which ordinarily could only be found in blues improvisation."
It is the spirit of the itinerant musician that Marshall was able to
capture and put into his rags.

Before the law forced Marshall to enroll his daughter, Mildred,
in school, she received her education in the minstrel shows and
districts where he played. She still remembered in a July 1975
interview the free and exciting life of those days:

> I know one thing: When I used to horse around and Papa
> would be working up and down the strip, Pop could have had
> fifty thousand women if he wanted to, 'cause I was right there
> with him and I know. You take a piano player like that—
> unless his wife is right along with him—well, that's life—that's
> music—it's that kind of world, baby! I'm not going to lie.
> Sure, my old man was a swinger, and he was in show life—he
> wrote MUSIC! But it's a wonderful life. If I ever hear anyone
> talkin' that show life, show people aren't any good, I'll knock
> 'em right down!!

Marshall lived until 1968 without ever making a commercial
recording. The one record he did make, a home recording done in
1956, was unintentionally destroyed in 1975 by the United States
Postal Service while it was in transit to Columbia Records for
copying. (For that loss you may blame this author for not having
sense enough to pack the thing securely. I did, however, get a
chance to hear most of it before it was sent, and about ten seconds
worth of the record still remains intact.) "Little Jack's Rag," which
Marshall wrote, was recently discovered by Mildred Steward, who
was kind enough to allow its publication here for the first time.
The music follows.

James Scott is the second and, for me, the most mysterious
composer of what Rudi Blesh has called the big three classic-rag
writers (the third being Joseph Lamb). I say mysterious because
so little is known about him; we have only a very sketchy picture
of his life. We know that he was a black man from Carthage,
Missouri; he was a child prodigy having had two of his rags published by the time he was seventeen; and he probably studied
with Scott Joplin around 1905. Beyond that we are pretty much

LITTLE JACK'S RAG BY ARTHUR A. MARSHALL

left with the music, some thirty rags published between 1903 and 1922 mostly by John Stark. Among these are some extremely difficult pieces.

Scott's rags are quite fully chorded and riddled with difficult leaps for both hands. He was fond of such devices as introducing a motif and then quickly echoing it an octave up, all of this on top of an uncompromising "boom-chick" left hand. Also, the tunes do not come off unless they are played at a fairly bright tempo. Their execution demands a great deal of brilliance, flash, and strength from the pianist. Consequently, while many ragtime pianists admire Scott's work, few can play them properly. However, despite their musical complexity, there is rarely anything one could call revolutionary to be found in these rags.

James Scott was the master craftsman of the form rather than the creative artist. The mood and style of his 1903 rags is the same as in those of the 1920s. The only thing that changed through the years was the complexity; they became increasingly dense and difficult to master but never broke new ground like the Joplin rags. And also unlike the Joplin rags, they rarely contain dramatic emotional changes. Whereas Joplin might have placed a whole theme in a minor key, as in the second and fourth strains of "Magnetic Rag," James Scott would switch back and forth between major and minor, creating tension between the two in the same theme but rarely allowing the melancholy mood to be fully expressed.

There are a couple of other facts about Scott that are interesting. First, Rudi Blesh reported that he sat rigidly without moving his body when playing the piano. Second, Scott reportedly sent in his manuscripts to Stark untitled. All of this would further indicate that he took an intellectual and unemotional approach to his music. For this reason his rags seem consistently to lend themselves especially to the machinelike interpretation of the player piano.

Paradoxically, in spite of their apparently pianistic intent, Scott's rags have long been a favorite of traditional jazz bands. In the 1930s Jelly Roll Morton recorded, with full ensemble, Scott's "Hilarity Rag" and "The Climax Rag"; Turk Murphy, one of the founders of the jazz revival of the 1940s, has done likewise. Turk finds James Scott to be "the most exciting of the classic rag composers," and adds:

> Scott Joplin wrote and performed the very, very classic ragtime, where, you might notice, the leaning we've had would be toward the slightly jazzy side, and actually, I think that James Scott was a little more flamboyant than Scott Joplin— and in playing this way, he also wound up sounding a little jazzy, actually.

Ironically, John Stark, in his later desperate battle for the preservation of classic ragtime, titled one of James Scott's 1921 compositions "Don't Jazz Me—Rag (I'm Music)."

Joseph Lamb is the most curious and possibly the "purest" of the classic-rag composers. He was a white man from Brooklyn, New York, who never set foot in the Mississippi Valley where classic ragtime was born but nevertheless set out to write rags in the style of Scott Joplin. Fortunately, he had a chance to meet the master in person in 1907.

The meeting took place in John Stark's New York office, where Lamb's interest in the classic rags had made him a regular visitor. On this occasion he casually mentioned that Scott Joplin was one man that he would like to meet. Joplin happened to be sitting in the office and soon after their introduction invited Lamb over to his boarding house to play a couple of rags that he had written. Lamb played his "Sensation Rag" for Joplin, and to his great pleasure, at the conclusion Joplin complimented him, calling it a "real, colored rag." Shortly thereafter Joplin arranged to have Stark publish the rag but with his own name added as arranger to bolster sales. Thus Lamb's career as a composer was launched.

From 1908 to 1919 Stark published a dozen of Lamb's ragtime gems, and on the basis of these alone his place in the ragtime hall of fame would have been secured. In 1949, however, Joe began a second career, thanks to his rediscovery by Rudi Blesh and Harriet Janis. Through their combined efforts and those of several others, notably Bob Darch and Sam and Ann Charters, Lamb was encouraged not only to compose but also to organize many of his old manuscripts. Although not a performer, he was also persuaded by the Charters to record an album for Folkways Records shortly before his death in 1960 (see Discography). This remains one of the few recorded documents of the classic-rag composers.

Lamb was a completely committed follower of Joplin and in some ways takes up where Joplin leaves off. Joplin spent his life taking ragtime music out of a strictly performance-oriented entertainment tradition, shaping it into a composer's art form. This was a fight for Joplin—but Lamb took Joplin at his word and simply worked within the idiom as outlined by Joplin. He only knew classic ragtime as a published form of piano music. Lamb had no axe to grind. He wasn't proving the respectability of ragtime— he took it for granted—and he was thrilled at the chance to be published among those that he already admired in the field.

Lamb, in addition to being isolated from the Negro folk tradition of the Midwest, was also isolated from the economic struggles

Joe Lamb in 1959, shortly before his death

of the publishing business. Music was never an economic necessity with him but always a sideline; therefore he never encountered the need to compromise that plagued other composers. He simply wrote rags the way he heard them and the way he thought they should be written, according to the classic-rag aesthetic as set down by Joplin and Stark. It was enough for him to see his rags in print just the way he composed them. Only John Stark would have aided such an unprofitable venture.

Curiously, in 1959, when Ann Charters played several of Lamb's compositions for him, including "Ethiopia," he said that it was the first time he had ever heard it played by anyone but himself. One wonders how many people actually mastered the rags at the time of their original publication during the ragtime era.

The best of Lamb's rags are intricate, graceful, and melodic pieces of music that often bear a close resemblance to the best of the Joplin rags. In fact, Lamb was in a way like the ideal Scott Joplin: a man fully satisfied, exploring the intricate possibilities of the multipartite rag form without the obsession to move on to the "legitimacy" of the opera stage.

Lamb was very much his own man, however, as evidenced by the fact that he so quickly embraced this Negro music that was so foreign to his physical environment. And his rags are totally original. They are full of warmth, wistfulness, and invention that spring from pure musical fascination.

Perhaps in somewhat simplistic terms Joe Lamb can be seen as having completed the cycle of the classic rag that Scott Joplin had set in motion. Joplin was a revolutionary who took folk ragtime and created a new category of music by combining it with classical musical concepts. James Scott, a man of similar geographic and racial background, worked within the guidelines set out by Joplin for the classic rag and, in effect, replicated the experiment. Then Lamb came from an entirely different background and took the results of Joplin's experiments as an accomplished fact, and in doing so he confirmed the success of Joplin's vision.

There were a number of other writers of the classic rag that have not been discussed in this chapter, but the men whose stories have been briefly covered here seem to be the important pioneers. Without them the whole "fragile" concept of the classic rag would not have survived. Even as it was, the music only barely escaped oblivion.

John Stark, after more or less failing in New York, returned to St. Louis and continued to increase his catalogue of classic rags until the 1920s, but it was a lost cause. What the public knew as ragtime was coming from the large commercial publishing houses of Tin Pan Alley.

4

Commercial Ragtime

Before 1900 it was still possible for nearly anyone to get into the music-publishing business. There were hundreds of small publishers spread throughout the United States. A man like John Stark could begin somewhere out in the Midwest with a piece of music like the "Maple Leaf Rag" and a handpress and within a few years have a million-selling international hit on his hands. But as much as anything else, the timing of its initial publication accounted for its phenomenal success. Stark probably never realized to what extent he had actually lucked out with the "Maple Leaf"; Joplin may have been writing for the ages, but the country was particularly ripe for his masterpiece in 1899. Joplin and Stark never really had their fingers on the musical pulse of the land; rather, they were involved with a timely fad that eventually wore off.

Stark made a fatal commercial error in his inflexible support of classic ragtime; and it was fortunate for us that he did. Otherwise we wouldn't have the music that has survived solely through his efforts. Nonetheless, a great deal of music that was published by Stark and Son was not up to snuff, and his categorical rejection of other musical innovations, such as jazz, really puts him in the same category as the stuffed shirts he was fighting against for the acceptance of ragtime.

Having said all this, however, I still can't go very far in commending the greedy opportunists who have, by and large, represented the music business in the United States. Music became commercialized during the Gilded Age (the Gay Nineties), at the same time as the other monolithic enterprises that shape and control every other facet of life were gaining a strong economic and philosophic foothold on the country. To see the song industry, then, is to see the whole economic system in microcosm. And make no mistake about it, never in the history of man was there ever a better opportunity for men bent on the accumulation of wealth to accomplish their desires.

THE MUSIC INDUSTRY

The song industry operated on the same premises as any other big business: It said, "We are giving the public what it wants," but it came to operate by the monopolistic practice of giving the public what it could be *made* to want.

The commercial potentialities of the song business began to be realized in the 1880s, when a number of ambitious young men began hitting on ideas for "selling" their songs. This was the beginning of a transformation of the music-publishing business from a rather docile, conservative animal into an aggressive beast. The first "sign of the times" appeared on the door of Charles K. Harris:

CHARLES K. HARRIS
BANJOIST AND SONG WRITER
SONGS WRITTEN TO ORDER

The last line is the key—music, rather than flowing from abstract artistic inspiration or folk sources, is here seen as a commodity to be manufactured, advertised, bought, and sold like any other product. In 1894 Harris produced the first million-selling piece of sheet music, "After the Ball,"* and in so doing, demonstrated the efficacy of mass public exposure. The song, which tells the sad story of lifelong frustrated love, was introduced into the popular show *A Trip to Chinatown* in 1892 and then a year later was played extensively at the Chicago World's Fair by John Philip Sousa, who continued to perform it at nearly every concert for the

---

* Not to be confused with the "Maple Leaf Rag," which was the first *instrumental* million seller.

next ten years. Within a few years Harris had sold over five million copies of his song. He was not, however, the only musical salesman in the field.

By the 1890s there came to be a number of sharp, young, highly competitive and opportunistic publishers congregated in small offices in the music capital of the United States, New York City. The scene was first centered around Times Square, then later shifted to a strip on Twenty-eighth Street between Fifth Avenue and Broadway. This was the locale for what was known as Tin Pan Alley, although the name came to apply to the entire music-publishing industry.

The name seems to have been coined by Monroe Rosenfeld, sometime song writer, journalist, and local character, who thought the sound of the battered uprights in the various offices on the strip sounded like falling tin pans. The title not only caught the spirit of the music but also the flavor of the life-style: It was a brash, jangling atmosphere of competition in which only the toughest and most durable publishers survived. Their success depended upon their ability to capitalize on every means available of getting their music before the public, and so they were quick to utilize the latest inventions to sell their tunes. In a very short time they moved from live music to piano rolls to phonograph records to radio.

These various media produced great changes in the way people heard music. And in a very real sense, as Marshall McLuhan has shown, the media determined to a large extent both the form and content of the music. No one has been more aware of this than the professionals of Tin Pan Alley.

THE MEDIA

The commercial ragtime era began in the 1890s, when live music was the norm. There was as yet no means of reproducing the performances in a more permanent form. The publishers had to rely on direct performer-audience communication for publicizing their wares—simple word of mouth. Their representatives were those highly energetic tune salesmen called pluggers, who would visit beer halls, picnics, restaurants, theaters—anywhere songs were sung—and make sure that their employers' tunes were part of the repertoire. Typically, a plugger might visit as many as sixty beer halls and variety houses within a week for this purpose. For the price of a round of beers he could get the orchestra to play his tune, and he himself might sing it; the second chorus would be whistled; and by the third chorus the audience, having been supplied with chorus slips (the printed words to the song) would be joining in and by then would have the tune firmly embedded in their minds.

Of course, as competition increased, the performers became more important to the publishers, and it became the pluggers' job to entice them by whatever means to perform the company songs. At first the pluggers hung around the theaters in order to get the singers to do their numbers, but as the mutually beneficial relationship between performers and publishers became apparent, it became more common for the stage people to come to the "music parlors" of the publishers, where with the help of a staff pianist they would be trained in the new material that was to be put in their shows. For this the singer would often not only be immortalized with his or her picture on the cover of the sheets, along with the words "as performed successfully by," but also paid outright by the publisher.

Note: The music was not sold to entertainers. The buyers were the people who would play it on their own pianos, and in the 1890s every respectable home in the country had a piano in the salon, the home entertainment center. But who played them? The ladies, of course.

The pop tunes of the 1890s may have been composed by male writers who lived in the rough-and-tumble, vice-ridden bowery, but their intended audience was those ladies of Victorian moral persuasion who bought the music. The result was a concentrated, hypocritical appeal to the hidden frustrations of these highly repressed females. There were endless numbers of poignantly pathetic ballads about unrequited love, tragic death, and ruined women. As one writer cynically put it, "Half of them wanted to be led astray—the other half wanted to read about it." Tin Pan Alley gave them what they wanted: escape music derived not from daily life but from superficial myths, dreams, and desires.

Ragtime music, coming in the middle of the 1890s, had a sales potential as sheet music for the home piano, but that alone does not account for its astounding success. As a kind of dream music its primitive, earthy syncopations provided an escape from the realities of industrialization. The country was becoming urbanized, but ragtime, with its "coon song" imagery, spoke of the simple life of the rural southern Negro and in its rhythm suggested the bodily movement of the dance. Joplin and a few other black composers had a direct contact with that life, but their attempts to portray it in any realistic manner invariably met with failure. In an age when mechanization and job security were becoming primary concerns, the carefree Negro of an earlier age, dancing and singing ragtime down on the plantation, was a comforting image.

The inventions of the industrial age provided the means of dissemination of ragtime, and, conversely, ragtime was geared to the needs of the inventions. Consider the phonograph record.

Edison's cylinder machines, which dominated the market before 1900, were mechanical devices whose speed was extremely variable and whose peculiar acoustics cut out a great deal of the

Sousa's U.S. Marine Band at a recording session in 1891. Library of Congress.

sound spectrum. Owing to these dictates only certain voices and instruments could be used. A further difficulty was the inability to mass-produce the cylinders. In the very early days the machine used to play back was the same one that recorded: A large wooden horn would capture the sound and transfer it acoustically to a stylus that would cut the performance into wax from the direct impulses of the sound. Although they developed a system whereby one horn could feed up to seven machines, a performer still had to make twenty to forty separate performances in a day to produce two hundred or so cylinders.

The piano recorded very poorly on these machines, but an instrument like the banjo was in great demand; its punchy, fast-decaying sound minimized the defects of the recording process. Vess Ossman, "the banjo king," and others like him became recording stars because they were able to turn in consistent work, without mistakes, that conformed perfectly to the allotted time of the record. If a number ran over, they would simply play it faster. Payment was made according to the number of runthroughs.

It was a great breakthrough when Emile Berliner later introduced the flat disc, which could be mass-produced. It was also stable enough to allow for piano recordings, but few appeared until 1912. None of the great classic-rag composers are known to have recorded during the ragtime era, and it is perhaps just as well that they didn't. It wasn't their medium; for as we've seen, musical artistry was strictly secondary to the needs of the machine; the correct tempo became the one that completed the tune in the necessary two-minute time slot; the correct dynamics were those that made an imprint in the wax with the least distortion.

Yet, in spite of these limitations, there are a number of early ragtime recordings that are well worth listening to today. There were quite a few brilliant technicians, such as Vess Ossman and Fred Van Eps on banjo, George Hamilton Green and Eli Cota on xylophone, and Guido and Pietro Deiro on accordion, and many of the recordings of the era are fascinating in their methods of building musical productions under such restrictive conditions.

The most important medium in terms of the instrumental rag, however, was the player piano. If ragtime was a transferring of folk themes into the rigid medium of printed music, then the player piano was a logical extension, for it further locked in the

subtle syncopations that had previously been born of natural body movement and live performance.

The player piano, as a forerunner to today's electronic synthesizers and multitrack tape recorders, could be used (even more than phonograph records, which still bore the "live" quality of their artists) to construct a perfect performance. And this is where the classic rags show up—often in improved form from their piano scores.

Before 1912 the process for making piano rolls was entirely mechanical. The roll arrangers would not play and have their performances transferred to rolls as they sometimes did in later years. Rather, they would construct a performance mathematically: The piano roll consists of vertical slits in a long paper roll, each of which represents and activates a single note on the piano as it passes over the tracking device. The position of the slit on the paper, from left to right, determines which note is played, and the length of the slit corresponds to the duration of the note. The later rolls, usually labeled "hand played," were constructed by means of a mechanism that inked onto paper an impression of the sounds created by a live performance. This "master" could then be edited, modified, corrected for mistakes, and "beefed up" with additional notes.

Each roll company would try to make its versions different from its competitors' by adding frills. These counter melodies, doubled octaves, tremolos, rapid chromatic runs, and the like—all impossible to play by hand—were so effective in the rags that I think it becomes necessary to view these arrangers as at least partly responsible for their success. In any case, we know that many rags were conceived by these arrangers in larger terms than the piano scores indicate. In later years some of the piano-roll arrangers emerged with their own distinct style of ragtime based on these pianistic devices, which they called novelty piano.

Ragtime purists have denigrated the piano-roll stylists such as Phil Ohman, Frank Banta, Felix Arndt, and Charlie Straight as being responsible for the destruction of "real" ragtime. This does not seem to be the case. Max Kortlander, in fact, who made a number of hand-played rolls for the Q.R.S. roll company, was one of the few performers of Joseph Lamb's rags, and he himself composed a number of rags in the classic "slow drag" vein.

These men did not degrade the rag. What they did do, however, was to take ragtime in its abstract essence as piano-roll music and expand it. Developing a whole system of conventions, often based on the harmonic concepts of the Impressionists, they produced a unique style and body of music that became at least as fully realized as the classic rag.

Although their stylistic devices, such as sliding block chords, tone clusters, augmented chords, and the like, had begun to ap-

Page from Zez Confrey's *Modern Course in Novelty Piano Playing* (1923) with endorsements by a host of novelty pianists.

pear in piano rolls earlier, the novelty style became officially recognized with the publication by Mills Music of six numbers by Zez Confrey in 1921. These highly pianistic pieces included "My Pet" and the enormously popular "Kitten on the Keys." (Note the reference to the piano in the title. There are no such references in Joplin.)

Another important composer in the genre was Roy Bargy, who wrote one novelty rag per month for piano-roll distribution in 1919. These include the remarkable "Jim Jams" and "Knice and Knifty."

There was a whole body of piano literature published in this style by various composers, mostly during the 1920s, but like the older ragtime, it has suffered from neglect. Much of it has still not been rediscovered or evaluated by musical scholars. Mills Music, which published a great amount of it, no longer even has file copies of most of it, and, in fact, threw away without publication a whole series of novelty-rag manuscripts written by Joe Lamb. Zez Confrey died in 1971, having been only briefly interviewed by one contemporary scholar, David Jasen. But there is one saving grace: At least in the case of novelty rags we have recorded documents that allow us to hear the style as it was played, in most cases, by the composers.

SHOW BIZ

Ragtime was first introduced and generally conceived by the public as a style of playing rather than a genre of composition. As early as 1897 Ben Harney issued his *Ragtime Instructor*, which demonstrated how nearly any piece of music could be ragged. And several years later Axel Christensen developed a whole network of ragtime schools based on this precept.

Most ragtime scholars have tended to say that white ragtime was primarily involved with this ragging of straight melodies, whereas the black approach was to think of tunes that were syncopated in their conception. At best, this is an oversimplification. Even ignoring the fact that Ben Harney was at least partly Negro, it must still be admitted that the early black folk-ragtime players ragged all the tunes they heard. Eubie Blake has recounted how the first ragtime he ever heard was from bands ragging the standard march music, and he himself has turned many classics and pop tunes into rags. Even Scott Joplin sanctioned this principle in print, in his endorsement for one of the white ragtime schools.

There was, however, what you might call a "show-biz" version of ragtime, which, growing out of vaudeville, leaned heavily on the more novel aspects of the music. One favorite trick of some performers, notably Mike Bernard, was to play one tune with the right hand and another tune simultaneously with the left. Jay Roberts wrote this into his very popular "Entertainer's Rag" (not to be confused with Scott Joplin's "The Entertainer"), which featured the simultaneous rendition of "Yankee Doodle" and "Dixie."

THE ENTERTAINER'S RAG

Axel Christensen, in response to a request for one of his typical 1915 programs, listed the following, which included "The Entertainer's Rag":

Just now I open my act with "I'm a Long Way From Tipperary," (in ragtime of course). This is followed by a syncopated version of the overture "Tannhäuser." The "Entertainer's Rag" is next. Then a medley of popular melodies in various styles of ragtime, among which is a waltz rag arrangement of "When You and I Were Young Maggie." For encores I use a recitation-pianologue, entitled the "Girl I Kissed on the Stairs," impersonations of Bert Williams, etc.*

Christensen lists (1) a pop song played in ragtime; (2) a classic played in ragtime; (3) a popular, flashy rag of the day; (4) a medley of popular melodies, including a waltz, played in ragtime; (5) a recitation-pianologue; and (6) impersonations of Bert Williams. One thing that immediately strikes me about this program is how much it resembles part of Eubie Blake's repertoire. A typical Blake program might include (1) "Alexander's Ragtime Band," a pop tune; (2) "Tannhäuser," which he also has arranged in ragtime; (3) "Tricky Fingers," a flashy rag; (4) "The Merry Widow," a waltz played in ragtime; (5) the story of the first time Eubie ever heard ragtime, a recitation-pianologue; and (6) "He's Just a Cousin of Mine," a Bert Williams imitation.

This was show business, not simply "white ragtime." Even James P. Johnson, the great Negro stride piano player, had a number in which he played "Dixie" with one hand and "The Star-Spangled Banner" with the other.

STAFF ARRANGERS

By far the largest volume of instrumental ragtime produced during the era was composed by the staff arrangers who were employed by the various publishing houses. And in evaluating the scores of all the rags, we have to consider the arranger's influence

---

* Axel Christensen, *Christensen's Ragtime Review* (Chicago), July 1915, p. 28.

on the form, for it was his job to make all published music interesting in a variety of instrumentations. For example, the cover of Tom Turpin's "Bowery Buck" states that it is available not only for piano but also for mandolin solo; two mandolins; one mandolin, guitar, and piano; two mandolins, guitar, and piano; mandolin and guitar; two mandolins and guitar; banjo; two banjos; orchestra; and band.

The published rag was not just piano music. In fact, the best arrangers made it a point not even to use a piano in their work. J. Bodewalt Lampe, composer of many rags and cakewalks and chief arranger for Remick Music, made the observation in 1917 that there was, in fact, no piano in the Remick arranging department because "a thorough knowledge of harmony is necessary to the well equipped arranger, and he must not be obliged to continually refer to the piano or any other instrument. . . . An arranger should be . . . theoretically at least, familiar with all the instruments."*

The result of this type of arrangement conception is that many rags cannot be fully appreciated in their simplified piano versions but come to life when played in full orchestration or by way of the more complete piano roll.

It is interesting to note that the piano roll of Joplin's "Pineapple Rag" was played in the same key (D) as the stock orchestration. This indicates that the roll arranger probably used the full-orchestration arrangement rather than the piano music (in B♭) as a model, and the roll thus contains a much thicker texture and duplicates more parts of the orchestra than would be possible in a hand-played performance. The question arises, Did Joplin conceive of the piece in this fuller version or in the more simplified piano-score version? There is no way of knowing, but it's quite possible that Joplin himself orchestrated the rag.

Very little research has been done in this area because of the scarcity of surviving orchestrations. The piano scores are common owing to the large number of pianos in the country, but the music for the orchestra, although just as important, simply doesn't turn up as much. From material we do have available, it appears that the art of arranging rags for band and orchestra was greatly per-

---

*Reprinted from an article in a 1917 copy of "Tuneful Yankee." J. Bodewalt Lampe, "The Art of Arranging Music," *Rag Times*, 7, no. 5 (January 1974): p. 5.

fected during the ragtime era. We need only look at the work of such men as Harry Alford, who orchestrated Joplin's "Magnetic Rag" in 1914, to see great strides made in this area. Where earlier orchestrations, such as those of the Joplin pieces contained in the *Red Back Book of Rags* from 1905, were merely simple transcriptions of the rags, the arrangements made less than a decade later show a regard for the unique possibilities of the fuller ensemble form. This was not a static art.

SONG WRITERS

Although none of the composers of Tin Pan Alley limited themselves strictly to ragtime, for they were above all adaptable and wrote all manner of tunes, several of them wrote enough rag material for us to be able to classify them as rag writers. And in spite of the negative aspects of their conformity to public expectations, there were still a few of the group who demonstrated remarkable genius in their profession. They did sometimes reflect the healthier aspects of America's beliefs, and for this these great musical craftsmen of Tin Pan Alley deserve to be remembered kindly. Their greatest contribution would have to be the rag song, a hybrid form that combined a catchy theme, somewhat diluted Negro syncopation, and sometimes extremely clever lyrics. Although most of the greatest Alley writers were surprisingly weak in music theory (many could only play in one key and most knew little about chords), they had the knack of being able to construct the famous "melody you can whistle." There were perhaps thirty or so composers who made significant contributions, but I think three men, Harry von Tilzer, George M. Cohan, and Irving Berlin, warrant special attention.

Harry von Tilzer became by 1900 the first established master of the art of satisfying, forecasting, and shaping public taste in music. Using a "scatter-shot" approach to song writing, the extremely prolific von Tilzer cranked out hundreds of tunes every year, a fair percentage of them hits. His main asset, however, was his flexibility.

Von Tilzer began as a successful ballad writer during the 1890s, but unlike many of his contemporaries, he did not become hope-

lessly mired in drippy sentiment. For in addition to turning out the ballads such as "A Bird in a Gilded Cage," he was able to produce syncopated hits like "What You Gonna Do When the Rent Comes Round (Rufus Rastus Johnson Brown)" and "Movin' Day."

In the theater, the most important tunesmith of these early days was the indomitable George M. Cohan. Cohan, who was the star, composer, lyricist, librettist, director, and producer of most of his shows. He relied heavily on tunes reflecting the nationalistic optimism of the times, such as "I'm a Yankee Doodle Dandy" and "You're a Grand Old Flag" (originally "You're a Grand Old Rag"), but his shows also contained a healthy smattering of syncopation in the form of ragtime weddings and ragtime court trials.

Cohan was, in his heyday, a practical song writer. During the opening nights of his shows he would listen at intermission and see which melodies the audiences were whistling. If no one remembered a tune, it was dropped and another was put in. Using this formula, Cohan dominated the musical stage with his self-confident Americanism for the first decade of the century. But then, like many other composers who lasted for a time and then faded, Cohan in the final analysis failed to adapt to the changes in public taste. The breezy flag-waving extravaganzas that made him famous appeared dated after World War I to the new, sophisticated jazz-age theatergoers, and he never recovered his momentum.

Throughout the ragtime era there were always rumors that ragtime was dying, and indeed for it to have lasted such a long time (over twenty years) it needed to be revitalized from time to time. The age of von Tilzer and Cohan had nearly come to a close when Irving Berlin grabbed the stage in 1911 with "Alexander's Ragtime Band." With this number he not only gave ragtime a shot in the arm but also set in motion a dance craze that would continue in various forms from the grizzly bear, to the bunny hug, right into the jazz age that would follow.

Berlin was born in Russia in 1888. His father died when Irving was eight, and he was brought to this country at the age of ten. At fourteen he ran away to the Bowery, where he scrambled for change as a street singer. From there, through sheer effort and raw nerve, he worked his way into the song business. By teaching himself to play piano in one key—F♯—and working during the night on his songs, he had managed by 1911 to work his way into full partnership in Ted Snyder's publishing firm and had more than fifty tunes to his credit. By 1914, he was writing a full score for the musical *Watch Your Step*, which established him not only in the song-writing business of Tin Pan Alley but also in the world of the musical theater.

Berlin's genius lies in two areas: first, his ability to tap the nostalgic, sentimental (actually, the self-pitying) strain of the

1915 Irving Berlin hit

American collective consciousness; and second, his simple ingenuity in constructing a song. Berlin articulated the common Tin Pan Alley belief that there are no new songs, only new ways to put themes together. The trick, as he explained it, was to give the public something slightly different than what it is expecting—a new twist on an old theme.

. . . and if you want to hear that Swanee River played in
    ragtime,
Come on and hear. . .

                           "Alexander's Ragtime Band"

Scott Joplin was years ahead of his time—but Berlin led the
parade from his position only a few steps ahead. Berlin is probably the best composer that Tin Pan Alley has produced. As
Jerome Kern has said, "Irving Berlin has no place in American
music; he is American music."*

* Michael Freedland, *Irving Berlin* (New York: Stein and Day, 1974),
p. 12.

5

Black Music in the East

BLACKS ON STAGE

The movement toward national recognition of Negro folk music that had first stirred at the Chicago World's Fair of 1893 found its logical home in New York City, the entertainment capital of the United States. So it was here that the top Negro musical artists began to congregate in the early part of the century and direct their efforts toward the goal of building Negro folk music into a national and international music with its own peculiar harmonies, instrumentation, and technical style.

The philosophy behind the movement probably could be traced to Booker T. Washington, who spoke for most of the black intellectual community. It was his belief that his people could improve their position only with the consent of the white race, and therefore, Negroes should not struggle against the restrictions imposed upon them but rather earn approval by displaying industry, sobriety, competence, and obedience to their employers. (It should be noted that Washington was at that time in control of virtually all distributions of money by private philanthropy for the benefit of Negroes; his theory, however, probably represented a practical approach for the blacks of the period, at least in terms of the arts.)

The first goal of the movement was to break down and eliminate the pseudo-Negro imagery of the minstrel show and replace it with genuine ethnic material. In 1891 Sam T. Jack originated *The Creole Show*, which, although cast in the traditional minstrel format, broke with the burnt-cork tradition by glorifying the Negro girl. This all-black show played successfully in Boston and at the Chicago World's Fair, then toured for a total of six consecutive seasons. This was followed by a number of similar productions: *South Before the War, The Octoroons,* and *Oriental America.* In 1898 Bob Cole produced the first all-black musical comedy, *A Trip to Coontown.*

The first Negro musical comedy to actually play New York was the 1898 production of *Clorindy, or The Origin of the Cakewalk.* With words by the great black poet Paul Lawrence Dunbar, it featured a score by Will Marion Cook, who was considered by his peers to be the most original Negro musical genius of his day. He seems, however, to have been a bitter and frustrated man. A gifted musician who had studied music with the great European masters, such as Dvořák, he felt he had been denied the glory due him because of his color and, therefore, often took a strident attitude toward whites. Eubie Blake recalls:

"Will Marion Cook was the man who taught me how to conduct. He was the musical granddaddy of us all—but he was a very nasty man. I remember in 1902 he took me to Schirmer Publishers to try to sell my rag 'The Charleston Rag' (it had been named by James Reese Europe 'Sounds of Africa' at that time). Now, first of all I'll tell you—Schirmer didn't take any ragtime then. But we went in and I played 'The Charleston Rag' for a man in the office. His name was Kurt Schindler, and he was one of the finest gentlemen I have ever met. Now, I didn't know anything about composition—I didn't know you have to prepare the ear to change keys; you can't just jump into a new key. So this man says, 'Why do you go from D♭ right into G♭?' (He already had a check written for a hundred dollars advance royalty—that's like a thousand dollars today. I was going to give Cook twenty-five and keep seventy-five for myself.) Cook jumps in and says, 'What right have you to chastise my protégé?' (At that time I didn't even know what the word *protégé* meant.) The guy says, "I didn't chastise him—I just asked him!' Then Cook says, 'How long have you been a Negro?' He says, 'I've never been a Negro.' So Cook tells him, 'We don't tell you how to write *your* music and you don't tell us how to write *ours!*' The man never took the tune. Cook and I left that office and my first instinct was to knock him down when we got to Fifth Avenue, but I thought, no, I shouldn't do that, so I asked him, 'Why did you do that?' He says, 'Let me tell you something—never let these people run over you.' I said, 'The man has got what I want—money!'

"Cook was a great musician, but he tried to push things down people's throats. I think maybe he got that in Europe. He was trying to ape Richard Wagner."

In spite of his abrasive attitude, however, Cook accomplished a great deal. After his *Clorindy, or The Origin of the Cakewalk* he went on to write a number of other musical comedies that featured the considerable talents of Bert Williams and George Walker.

It was Williams and Walker who were responsible for reducing the minstrel show to a two-man act. Williams played the shuffling, slow, rural "Jim Crow" Negro and Walker the slick, well-dressed, urban "Zip Coon" character.

After Walker died in 1911, Williams went on to become probably the most popular Negro comedian of all time. But his story is a pathetic one, related to a common problem of all of these men.

Williams achieved amazing success. He and Walker starred in *Clorindy*, the first black show to play Broadway; he became the first black entertainer to break the color line and star in the *Ziegfeld Follies*; he attained a degree of comic artistry that has never been surpassed—but he did all of this portraying the epitome of the shuffling "coon." He hated the image, but he perpetuated it nevertheless. The incongruity of his situation made him a near-recluse all his life. A light-skinned West Indian who had to "blacken up" for the stage, he was never able to identify with the black race that he caricatured or the white from which he was naturally excluded. Williams was the very symbol of alienation—a man caught alone between cultures. In this sense he captured much of the spirit of ragtime. In what Duke Ellington has called "the twisted pathos" of his humor, Williams expressed the same sense of isolation that projected from the Scott Joplin rags.

Williams and his associate writers, Alex Rogers, Cecil Mack, and Chris Smith, turned out a number of fine songs. While many are within the context of the "coon song," a surprising number are much more universal and hold up well today. He is probably best remembered for his theme song, "Nobody," which expresses the essence of his characterization:

I ain't never done nothin' to Nobody;
I ain't never got nothin' from Nobody,
    no time;
And until I get somethin' from Somebody,
    some time,
I intend to do nothin' for Nobody,
    no time.

A Tin Pan Alley song made popular by Bert Williams, 1910

Williams died in 1922, leaving behind a number of recordings. Considered in context, they are well worth a listen for they reveal the high quality of his material and the subtlety and intricate sense of timing in Williams's delivery.

Another black entertainer–song writer to be caught in the same bind was Ernest Hogan, who was billed as "The Unbleached American." His early song, "All Coons Look Alike To Me," became the standard test piece for the numerous ragtime-piano contests held in the 1890s. Unfortunately, this song, which had very innocent lyrics, for its title alone became a symbol for racism and haunted him for the rest of his life.

If the work of these composers appears to be extremely derogatory today, consider the circumstances under which they were written. In order to make any changes blacks first had to get on the stage—only then could they work on eliminating the stereotypes and presenting Negroes in a truer light. But in 1900 they were not even permitted to express feelings of love on stage.

THE CLEF CLUB

The greatest force in organizing and channeling the efforts of black musicians in New York was James Reese Europe. Around 1911 he and several other well-educated black composers and players, which included Will Vodery, William Tyers, Ford Dabney, and Will Marion Cook, organized the Clef Club to represent and promote their interests. Under Europe's leadership, the organization was able to make great improvements in their working conditions.

The Clef Club musicians didn't dress in shabby outfits and work all night in dives; they wore tuxes, played regular hours set by contracts, and were well paid for their services. But above all, the Clef Club served to raise the image of the Negro musician and get him work in the highest social circles. Its members played for the superrich "blue bloods" of New York.

Although there were clearly a number of excellent players among the members, Europe managed to sell a great deal of entertainment on the strength of the mystique of colored music.

James Reese Europe and his Society Orchestra, ca. 1916

A few quotes from an interview he gave in 1914 describe his ideas on exclusivity.

> In playing symphonic music we are careful to play only the work of our own composers. I know of no white man who has written Negro music that rings true. . . .
>
> I would not permit my orchestra to play the compositions of white men because I know that my musicians could not begin to rival white men at interpreting the creations of white composers. . . . Music breathes the spirit of a race, and, strictly speaking, it is a part only of the race which creates it. . . .
>
> We colored people have our own music that is part of us; it's the product of our souls; it's been created by the sufferings and miseries of our race.*

Using this sort of justification, Europe assembled large Negro symphonic groups with sometimes extremely unusual and unwieldy instrumentation totally incapable of playing improvisation. One Clef Club orchestra contained fifty mandolins, twenty violins, thirty harp-guitars, ten cellos, one saxophone, ten banjos, two organs, five flutes, five bass violins, five clarinets, three timpani, ten pianos, and drums. Often in such ensembles many of the string players had to be taught how to play a few chords just to get through the evening or would, in fact, sometimes be holding dummy instruments with rubber strings. It was a case of "outguessing Mr. Eddie." The "upper 400" would always get their requested number of "genuine colored musicians," although some of those musicians could only sing.

Europe's efforts resulted in his musicians being the favorite accompanists for America's most popular dance team, Irene and Vernon Castle, and some of the dances that they popularized required ragtime music. Europe himself wrote "The Castle House Rag"; but the best rags to emerge from this scene were provided in 1914 by a couple of piano players from out of town: Luckey Roberts contributed "Junk Man Rag" and "Pork and Beans," and his friend from Baltimore, Eubie Blake, followed with "Chevy Chase" and "Fizz Water." Although these rags, especially in their published form, have an affinity to the classic rags, neither of these two men were rag writers in the Joplin sense. They had

* *Evening Post*, March 13, 1914.

CASTLE·HOUSE·RAG

FOX TROT

INTRODUCED BY
MR & MRS VERNON CASTLE

COMPOSED BY EUROPE OF EUROPE'S SOCIETY ORCHESTRA

absorbed the ragtime from the Midwest, but it was only part of their musical background; they had absorbed everything they could get their hands on. While Eubie, as was the custom in the early part of the century, refers, even as late as the 1970s, to *all* syncopated popular music as ragtime, he and his contemporaries were striving for something beyond the limits of the rag as defined by Joplin.

As New York stride pianist, Willie "The Lion" Smith put it:

> Ragtime means a guy that don't know the keyboard—he just rags off a few riffles what comes to him. He's bigoty and forward, very aggressive, until some guy comes in and calls his hand—then he pipes down like a lamb.
>
> Now, the difference between ragtime piano playing and a *pianist* [is that] a pianist is supposed to know all the progressions—how to move around with both hands. In case he's playing for a band or an entertainer and she gets sick, he has to be capable of singing, talking, playing, directing, and dancing.
>
> This [ragtime] was the style of piano they played when they didn't have good left hands. Now, that's what they call the corn. Some people think it's piano playing . . . that's pure corn! It means, "I don't know how to play." If I was playing the same thing, I'd stride it. There's your stride—it means "Real Good."*

Willie had a reputation for exaggeration, but he was right in this respect: *Stride*, which is the name of the piano style that emerged from the East Coast, was a good deal more forceful than the average ragtime piano style. It was strong, exhibitionistic, refined, and extremely challenging. While Joplin succeeded in getting his classic ragtime published as he conceived it, the East Coast "ticklers" rarely had their music transcribed in any form approaching its complexity in live performance. The word from the publisher was *simplify* so that the girl in the dimestore demonstrating the tunes on piano for prospective customers could cut it. So the practical demands of publishing took precedence.

* Willie "The Lion" Smith, *The Memoirs of Willie The Lion Smith* (New York: RCA, 1968), LPM 6016.

But we do have some recordings, and, most fortunately, a few of the pioneers have lived long enough to share their knowledge with this generation. And surely the most notable in this respect is the amazing Eubie Blake.

EUBIE BLAKE

For us today Eubie Blake is probably the most important of the East Coast ragtime/stride piano players for two reasons: first because of his phenomenal talent both as performer and composer; and second, because he has transmitted so much of his knowledge to our generation. Had it not been for Eubie surviving since before the turn of the century and remembering the early styles, we would know practically nothing about this important ragtime tradition.

Eubie was born in 1883 in the city of Baltimore, the son of former slaves. He learned a sense of humility through his very religious mother; and from his remarkable father, John Blake, he acquired an independence and humanity that have carried him through his ninety-plus years. In his own words:

> I'm proud of my mother and father—I loved them. I remember one Christmas my father called, "Em, have you got anything for that boy for Christmas?" She said, "Only what you brought in. . . ." 'Course, there wasn't nothin'. We didn't have any food. He kissed her—and that's the only time I ever saw them embrace—and he said, "If I don't come back, you tell your friends that a *man* went out to get something for his family to eat." He came back later with a wicker basket full of food—side of ham, large turkey, everything. I never forgot that.
>
> My father used to tell me, "If anybody does anything to you, you fight." He used to beat me for being afraid. I had to pass two white schools on my way to school, and naturally I was in fights all the time. I came in crying one time because I'd gotten whipped by some white boys. I said, "I hate white people." My father told me, "You don't hate all white people—only the people that did something to you." Today I believe that. You can't blame people for the way they were

raised. Some people were raised to think that colored people are no good—you can't blame them for that.

Eubie began playing the organ when he was six years old. He took lessons from their next-door neighbor but soon was adding his own syncopated variations.

One day my mother came home from work early and heard me playing like that. She said, "Take that ragtime out of my house!" That's the first time I ever heard the word *ragtime*.

Eubie made his first real contacts with the black ragtime players (or "jig piano" players, as they were then called) when he began a three-year engagement at Aggie Shelton's five-dollar (not cheap in those days) sporting house. Among this older generation of players that he heard were Will Turk, "Big Head" Wilbur, "Slue-Foot" Nelson, and Jesse Pickett, who composed a haunting tango-rag, "The Bull Dyke's Dream," which Eubie has preserved since the last century.

Eubie continued to absorb the music of the houses and dives for the next few years, but he also became greatly influenced by other types of music. In 1900 he was particularly taken by Leslie Stuart's *Florodora*, a light opera imported from England that featured a delightful sextet that moved through at least five different keys.* It became a challenge for the professors to be able to play it in any key. Eubie was so impressed that he decided he would try to write music like it, but he didn't have the chance until years later.

From 1907 to 1915 Eubie spent most of his time in Atlantic City, and it was during these years that he was, he feels, in his prime as a piano player. He would have to have been good, as he was working in the company of the finest players in the land, men such as James P. Johnson, Willie "The Lion" Smith, and Luckey Roberts who were just coming on the scene.

---

* This number was a special delight for the gentlemen of the audience; the Florodora Girls would play up to them, batting their big eyes and flashing come-hither smiles, often to find themselves the recipients of numerous gifts from rich "stage-door Johnnies." Many even ended up marrying their benefactors.

These were years of fierce competition among the piano players. They had to play well or they couldn't hold jobs. Musicians of all sorts would come in and hear them. They had to play everything—light opera, popular songs, and of course, dazzling rags. Scott Joplin's "Euphonic Sounds," which Eubie has called "a concerto for the left hand," was a popular test piece for the boys, and Eubie had his own specialties with which to demonstrate his technique, such as "Troublesome Ivories," "Tricky Fingers," and many more now lost because they were never written down.

> I was the first guy to have a rag based on scales. Eddy Clay-
> pool did it later, but I used to have a great arrangement—I've
> forgotten it now.
>
> I could play the piano then. I *knew* I could play. I had the
> strength and speed. . . . We used to start playing at nine o'clock
> and then play till we dropped dead in the morning. Then I'd
> stay up and play poker, and of course there were the girls. . . .
> Boy, I loved 'em. Well, you know how it is now—"the song is
> over but the melody lingers on."

Among the many luminaries who used to drop in and hear
Eubie was Irving Berlin.

> My partner, Madison Reed, and I made "Alexander's Ragtime
> Band" popular in Atlantic City in 1910. We got the profes-
> sional copy and played from that. Berlin used to come in with
> Sophie Tucker when she was in town and have us play it. Let
> me say one thing: If there ever was a musical *genius* in this
> country it was Irving Berlin—and he couldn't read a note. But
> he stood up there with Victor Herbert and Kern and the rest
> of them.

Eubie's own publishing career began in 1914 when Luckey
Roberts introduced him to the Joseph Stern Company. They published two of his rags, "Chevy Chase" and "Fizz Water."

> I still hardly ever play those two rags. You see, we were so
> anxious to get something published that we didn't read the
> fine print. I signed a contract that kept all the recording rights
> for the publishers. They used to do things like that to us—we
> didn't know any better. Another thing: Sometimes we'd go
> into a publisher's office and play a tune for them. They'd have
> a guy hidden who would take the number down and steal it.

In 1915 Eubie teamed up with lyricist Noble Sissle and in 1916
was persuaded to join him in New York to begin writing an all-
black Broadway show. The impetus for this venture came from
James Reese Europe. Then World War I hit, and plans for the
show had to be shelved. Europe and Sissle enlisted in the army

Eubie Blake, 1919.
Photograph by Ed
Lawless.

and formed an all-Negro, regimental band. Meanwhile Eubie, who was too old to be in the army, stayed in New York and took care of business for Europe. Finally, in 1919, the armistice was signed and the show's production could have progressed but for the death of Europe, who was stabbed by one of his drummers. Without Europe's guiding hand, the roof caved in on the whole project. And so Eubie went into vaudeville with Sissle.

Their act, "The Dixie Duo," was quite successful. After opening in Bridgeport, Connecticut, they were brought to the Harlem Opera House in New York City, then picked up by the Keith vaudeville circuit beginning with New York's prestigious Palace Theater. The record bears out that they stole the show every time.

It was the common practice of the times to have no more than one Negro act on a program, and so Sissle and Blake rarely worked with other Negro acts. However, in 1920 they were on the same program with the black comedy team Miller and Lyles. The eventual result of this encounter was the production of *Shuffle Along* in 1921. This musical comedy put blacks back on Broadway after a ten-year absence.

With *Shuffle Along* came Eubie's chance to write slower, more melodic numbers like the light-opera composers he loved. The big hit from the show, "I'm Just Wild About Harry," was, in fact, originally a waltz.

Eubie continued to infuse most of his music with ragtime, but the word fell out of use and he no longer composed rags. He did not return to the form until 1942. It was at that time that Eubie, retired from show business and breezing through a course in the Shillinger system of music (a four-year program that he completed in two years) composed "Dicty's on Seventh Avenue" as a demonstration of his understanding of modern musical principles.

During World War II Blake composed a number of shows for the USO, but then he once again retired until, in 1951, Rudi Blesh and Harriet Janis persuaded him to record and begin playing the old rags again. With their help and that of Bob Darch among others, Eubie launched a new career as the grandfather of ragtime piano.

In 1968 Columbia Records did a two-record set of Eubie's music (see Discography) that gave a great boost to his new career, and the early 1970s saw him once more writing rags, traveling the country, collecting awards, appearing on nearly every major talk and variety show on television, and with the help of Carl Seltzer, even starting his own recording company. And so this man, who was composing ragtime before the turn of the century, has brought the actual sound of that music to the ears of the 1970s generation.

Eubie Blake, in his long career, has written and played in a multitude of styles reflecting his vast musical exposure. But as he says, "I take a man's music and play it *my* way." In his way, Eubie has transformed classics, like the "Pilgrim's Chorus" from *Tannhäuser* and Christian Sinding's *Rustles of Spring*, as well as show

Eubie Blake in the early 1970s. Photograph by Ed Lawless.

tunes of later composers like Cole Porter into syncopated master-pieces. Ragtime, however, is only a part of his bag, and I would hope that anyone investigating his music would not merely con-centrate on the rags alone. There is in his work a wealth of inven-tiveness that often defies categorization. Call it ragtime, jazz, show tunes, classical, or whatever—it's all damn good music, and the incredible variety is one of its great strengths. Eubie's all-encompassing style is pure theater, the result of years of experi-ence in relating to audiences on a personal level. To understand

Eubie's music is to see him bounding on stage at the age of ninety like a man half that age; to see him strain with every ounce of his one hundred twenty-five pounds to get that piano to "talk" to an audience. He loves those people and his music shows it.

LUCKEY ROBERTS

Charles Luckeyth Roberts is one of those outstanding piano players and composers whose work has been all but lost. His only popular tune, "Moonlight Cocktail," was actually the first strain of a rag called "Ripples of the Nile." He was terribly underrecorded, unlike "Fats" Waller, James P. Johnson, and Eubie Blake, but his compositions for the piano are nothing short of astounding.

Roberts published two rags in 1913 that were brought out in connection with the dance vogues of the times, but both were drastically simplified—and herein lies the problem with most of his compositions: They were masterpieces but too sophisticated for the general public and almost impossible for anyone else to play. Luckey, as he was known, was the darling of high society for a number of years and a particular favorite of Franklin Roosevelt, but he only recorded his good material on two occasions, both late in his life. The first time was in 1946 when Rudi Blesh did a session for his Circle Records. Then in 1958, Good Time Jazz had him do six of his best numbers for an album, *Harlem Piano: Luckey and the Lion.* This last set of recordings is pure dynamite.

Roberts had tremendous power, overwhelming technique and ingenuity, and massive hands that could stretch a fourteenth. Like all the good stride players, his playing was based on a solid rhythmic left hand—but in the right he added ripping chromatic runs that often extended for three or four octaves at breakneck speed as well as a dramatic single-note drumming effect. Much of his music, heavily dependent upon performance, has been lost altogether, but one of his best compositions, the beautiful "Spanish Venus," has survived because of Eubie Blake's recollection of the tune. Eubie was probably Luckey's best friend and knew him better than anyone. Nat Hentoff, who supervised his last recording session, described Roberts in the liner notes as "one of the very few transparently honest men" he ever met.* But Eubie, who maybe had a clearer picture, says:

> Luckey was the biggest liar I've ever known, and he'd cheat at anything. He had tear-duct trouble and he could cry anytime he wanted to. He used to go over to a rough white section in Baltimore and play what we called lemon pool. He was a good pool player—a shark—but he'd pretend he couldn't play. If he ever got caught they'd have *killed* him—but he'd cry and talk his way out of anything.
>
> Of course, he was the strongest man I ever met. He was about as wide as that piano, and I never knew anybody to ever whip him.
>
> His dad and him used to think I was the king of England. He was from Philadelphia, but he ran away to Baltimore, where I was. I was only a few years older than him, but he was like a son to me.
>
> In the beginning he could only play in one key, F♯. He used to play for a singer; they'd say it was too high and he'd play the same thing an octave down.

George Gershwin was one of Roberts's pupils, and you can hear much of his teacher's influence, especially in Gershwin's earlier works. In fact, I played part of Gershwin's early rag, "Swanee Ripples," for Eubie and he was fairly certain it was one of Luckey's themes.

JAMES P. JOHNSON

James P. Johnson was unquestionably the finest exponent of stride piano, and in the sense that he consolidated a wide range of techniques and devices from disparate sources into one style that we now accept as the standard, he can be considered the father of stride piano.

---

* Nat Hentoff, *Harlem Piano: Luckey and the Lion* (Los Angeles: Good Time Jazz, produced by Contemporary Records, May 1960), S10035. From the liner notes.

Johnson was the master musician. He had perfect pitch and an imposing classical technique, but most of all, he had the ability and desire to assimilate from all types of music.

Jimmy's first music was ragtime, which was taught to him by his mother. Later he studied with an old European instructor, Bruto Gianinni, who, fortunately, allowed him to continue learning ragtime but insisted on correct fingering and a thorough schooling in music theory. Thus equipped, Johnson was able to observe all the finest Negro piano players on the East Coast, copy their best tricks, and combine them with an impressive array of concert effects. As Jimmy himself freely admitted: "I was getting around town and hearing everybody. If they had anything I didn't have—I listened and stole it."*

In his early years Johnson carefully studied the styles of Eubie Blake, Willie "The Lion" Smith, Luckey Roberts, and Jelly Roll Morton, and he picked up tricks from a host of professors whose names are all but forgotten today. From a legendary pianist by the name of Abba Labba he learned the walking bass, and he credits Fred Bryant with inventing the backward (descending) tenth, which became the keystone of his bass style. From all of these sources he distilled his own unique style of playing, which has had tremendous influence on numerous piano players ever since. Pianist Dick Wellstood has written:

> One of the most famous quotes of 1957 was the remark made by Thelonious Monk while he was listening to the playback of one of his solos: "That sounds like James P. Johnson." Strangely enough, Monk does sound like James P. from time to time, and so do Fats, Basie, Tatum, and Duke (as well as Willie Gant and Q. Roscoe Snowden). Since James P. has had such a strong influence on so many well-known pianists, it is amazing that . . . the average fan confuses him with Pete Johnson ("Do you really like boogie woogie?") and the average musician thinks of him affectionately, if dimly, as an early teacher of Fats Waller.
>
> James P. was not Pete Johnson, nor a mere "teacher" of Fats Waller. He was a much more interesting musician than Waller.

* Martin Williams, ed., *Jazz Panorama* (New York, London: Collier Books/Collier-Macmillan, 1964), p. 55.

His bass lines are better constructed, his right hand is freer and less repetitive, his rhythm is more accurate, and his playing is not so relentlessly two-beat as that of Fats. Although he lacked the smooth technique of Tatum (and of Fats) and the striking harmonic imagination of Ellington, he nonetheless carved out a style which was rich enough in general musical resources to have re-created at least fragments of itself in the playing of such unlike musicians as Monk and John Lewis.*

Unlike the introspective and restrained classic ragtime, Johnson's rags reflect his basically gregarious nature. He was attracted to the music because of the social contacts that it provided. Before World War I everyone had a piano, but few people could play it; so a piano player was important socially. Johnson played for the people—at rent parties, clubs, whorehouses,—and this contact is apparent in his best music. In fact, it is the hallmark of the stride school. Johnson described the approach:

> After your opening piece to astound the audience, it would depend on the gal you were playing for or the mood of the place for what you would play next. It might be sentimental, moody, stompy or funky. The good player had to know just what the mood of the audience was.**

Much of James P.'s music came from the dance. His famous "Charleston" was composed around 1913 for the dances he used to play in New York for the poor South Carolina blacks who had recently come to the city to work as longshoremen. Many of his finest rags, or shouts, including "Carolina Shout" and "The Mule Walk," were ragtime arrangements of cotillion dances that these people did.

Through the twenties and thirties Johnson was much in demand as a recording artist for piano rolls, recorded dates, and even a few films, but he maintained his common ties. "The Lion," "Fats" Waller, and he made the rounds of the Harlem rent parties, where piano players were the stars and their every move was a performance:

* Ibid., p. 44. Reprinted with permission of the author.
** Ibid., p. 61.

You had to have an attitude, a style of behaving, that was your personal, professional trade mark. . . . Every move we made was studied, practiced, and developed just like it was a complicated piano piece. . . . When you came into a place you had a three-way play. You never took your overcoat or hat off until you were at the piano. First you laid your cane on the music rack. Then you took off your overcoat, folded it, and put it on the piano, with the lining showing. You then took off your hat before the audience. Each tickler had his own gesture for removing his hat with a little flourish. . . . You took out your silk handkerchief, shook it out, and dusted off the piano stool. . . . Every tickler kept these attitudes. . . . They were his professional personality and prepared the audience for the artistic performance to come. I've watched high-powered actors today, and they all have that professional approach. In the old days they really worked at it. It was designed to show a personality that women would admire. With the music he played, the tickler's manners would put the question in the ladies' minds: "Can he do it like he can play it?"*

Johnson's later years saw him retire somewhat as an active performer and concentrate more on writing symphonic music in the Negro folk tradition. Because of his superior musicianship and active social involvement in ragtime and jazz circles, he would be the logical man to write such serious music—but he never achieved success in the venture. While George Gershwin built his career on this concept with such works as *Rhapsody in Blue* and Concerto in F, Johnson's *Harlem Symphony* and *Jasmine* (*Jazz-o-Mine*) Concerto have rarely been heard. There are many reasons given for this neglect, but I think that the most likely possibility seems to be that the pieces simply don't hold up. His 1929 work *Yamecraw—A Harlem Rhapsody*, which was made into a Warner Brothers short film in 1930, illustrates some basic weaknesses in the concept. It is described on the cover as "a genuine Negro treatise on spiritual, syncopated, and blues melodies expressing the religious fervor and happy moods of the natives of Yamecraw, a Negro settlement situated on the outskirts of Savannah, Georgia."

* Ibid., pp. 59–61. Reprinted with permission of the author.

What emerges is a collage of short themes that seem to be lifted out of context and lose all sense of spontaneity. The notes are there but the natural warmth and depth of the music is absent. It's like seeing scenes from a movie in the form of "previews of coming attractions"—intriguing, but somehow incomplete.

Where Johnson was at his best was as a performer of rags and stomps. His two recordings made for Brunswick in 1930 of "Jingles" and "You've Got to Be Modernistic" are masterpieces of Harlem stride and demonstrate his articulate, economical, resourceful, and driving style.

James P.'s protégé, Thomas "Fats" Waller, actually popularized stride piano more than Johnson himself did. However, while Waller wrote some numbers in the older "shout" style, such as "Handful of Keys," it was his pop music that sold.* When he began recording in 1929, ragtime was a thoroughly dead issue. There is a fine line between ragtime and jazz. James P. Johnson and "Fats" Waller are categorized in both camps. But I think Johnson's roots can be clearly traced to the ragtime era, while Waller's career seems to fall more clearly on the jazz side. In any case, "Fats" Waller, Duke Ellington, Art Tatum, and the other graduates of the stride school have been thoroughly covered in the jazz books. Suffice it to say that stride piano, which was basically a refinement and expansion of ragtime, survived as the cornerstone of most jazz piano styles until the bop experimenters of the 1940s, like Bud Powell, reduced the use of the left hand as a rhythmic foundation. However, the rhythms of the bop players bear a remarkable similarity to the classic rags. As Bob Wright has pointed out, the rhythmic pattern of a Scott Joplin number like "Paragon Rag" sounds just like a Max Roach drum solo from the 1950s.

---

* *Shout* was a term applied to many of James P. Johnson's rags that were written for the semi-religious "ring shout" dances of the southern Negroes. (See page 8).

6
The Ragtime Era
Continues

Although by absolute numbers most published rags came out of New York, especially in the later years of the ragtime era (after 1910) there was an incredible amount of material that sprang up from all parts of the country, and much of it was superior to the Tin Pan Alley product. Even now these vast quantities of rags have yet to be fully evaluated by ragtime scholars. Some of these thousands of writers were amateurs who had maybe only one good tune in them which they published in their own home town; then there is that mass of nomadic musicians who scattered their published works among a number of different firms. This is the sort of thing that makes poring over a stack of sheet music from this era so interesting. Nine-tenths of the stuff will generally turn out to be junk—but then that one obscure gem, written by some-body you've never heard of and published in some one-horse town, will show up and knock you over with its off-the-wall in-ventiveness.

So in this chapter, before we leave the ragtime era and move on to the revivals, we'll briefly explore some of the ragged trails that have fascinated me and maybe tie up a few loose ends of the continuing ragtime story.

MERGING TRADITIONS

Not surprisingly, as the ragtime craze progressed, the previously well-defined regional influences became less pronounced. There were still centers of concentrated musical activity, but

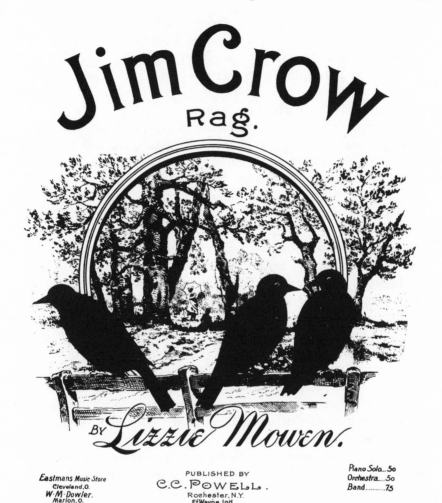

Jim Crow Rag.

By *Lizzie Mowen.*

Eastmans Music Store
Cleveland, O.
W·M·Dowler.
Marion, O.

PUBLISHED BY
C.C. POWELL.
Rochester, N.Y.
FtWayne, Ind.

Piano Solo....50
Orchestra.....50
Band............75

One of the many obscure rags from the heartland
of the United States

many of the published rags began to reveal a mixing of what
before had been localized styles.

As we have seen, the folk-classical ragtime that emerged from
the St. Louis area at the turn of the century was easily transport-
able because of its emphasis on the printed page of music and was
therefore very influential at least in the initial development of
ragtime styles throughout the country. However, during the

second decade of this century the regional flavor of other areas began to penetrate the works of the St. Louis musicians. In particular the St. Louis rags began to reflect a new sophistication and heartiness acquired through contact with the East Coast ticklers, as well as through blues and jazz tinges from New Orleans, Memphis, and other parts of the South.

Although there were undoubtedly many piano players whose playing style exemplified these eclectic trends, we will focus on two, Artie Matthews and Charlie Thompson, whose music has survived in either published or recorded form. The written music we do have of this particular phase of St. Louis ragtime is largely the work of Matthews, who, as the most musically literate composer in the area, not only wrote a magnificent set of rags himself but also transcribed for publication the music of several nonreading composers.

Matthews was the "musician's musician," whose performances often displayed a prodigious technique and a subtle sense of humor. His musical wit and intelligence are represented by a series of numbers called the "Pastime Rags," which were published by John Stark. We can only regret that there are but five of them. According to Rudi Blesh, who interviewed Artie in 1949, these were only part of a whole group of rags that he dashed off weekly for black variety shows. Matthews himself was so unconcerned about them that when Blesh talked with him, he was unaware that Stark had even published five of them. The remainder of the tunes were apparently thrown away. Actually he had only maintained and renewed the copyright to one of the Stark publications, and that was the popular "Weary Blues."

This brings us to a short discussion of blues. One might assume that the subject does not belong in a book on ragtime, but when the blues were first introduced to the general public around 1912, they were very much a part of the ragtime scene. Indeed, the two terms were often interchangeable. The "father of the blues," W. C. Handy, was often cited as a ragtime musician and in fact labeled several of his first published blues as rags. ("The Yellow Dog Blues" was, for instance, originally titled "The Yellow Dog Rag.") Blues were often simple twelve-bar rags, and as Handy's own early recordings indicate, they were not played at the slow tempo we commonly associate with blues but often at a bouncy,

Sheet music for W. C. Handy's first published blues. Note the label "a Southern Rag."

raggy clip. This overlapping relationship between blues and rags is further documented by a curious Scott Joplin piano-roll recording of a Handy number, "Ole Miss Rag," which could be mistaken for one of Joplin's own compositions.

Although Handy started the blues fad with his "Memphis Blues" in 1912, Artie Matthews actually beat him to the punch with his "Baby Seals Blues" published earlier the same year.

The blues-ragtime tradition also shows up in the works of Charlie Thompson, whose "Buffet Flat Rag" (or "Buffet Flat Blues") is a twelve-bar boogie-woogie rag. Thompson was one of those players who would have vanished into obscurity with only one number to his credit—his "Lily Rag" of 1914—if not for the fact that he did manage to make some records before his death in 1964. He appears on a few 78s in the 1940s, but an even better example of his work is included on the unfortunately now out-of-print *Golden Reunion in Ragtime* albums that Bob Darch produced in 1963 (see Discography). These were made when Thompson knew that he was dying of cancer and was anxious to make a last documentation of his playing. For me these are invaluable recordings because there is practically nothing else available to illustrate the St. Louis style of the time. Charlie's playing reveals his contact with James P. Johnson, whom he met around 1912, but it also clearly shows a jangling rhythmic independence between the two hands that I suspect was typical of the best St. Louis players. His recordings of the "Lily Rag" and "Delmar Rag" are particularly interesting in this respect.

Although there is little information available on them, there are a couple of other St. Louis composers of the period who appear in the Stark catalogue and should be mentioned here. These are Robert Hampton and Lucien Porter Gibson. Stark published Hampton's "Cataract Rag" and "Agitation Rag" in 1914 and 1915 respectively, and two Gibson works, "Jinx Rag" and "The Cactus Rag" in 1915 and 1916. "Jinx Rag" bears the inscription "Arranged by Artie Matthews," and I suspect that the others might also have been arranged by him, because there is a consistency of style among all four works that is somewhat similar to Matthews's own rags (though they are not as polished). This is one of many mysteries that emerge from Stark's catalogue. In addition to the confusion on arrangers, there is no way of really telling when the tunes were written. In one instance we know that the "Tom and Jerry Rag," which was published by Stark in 1917, was actually written in 1906. Publication of the "Pastime Rags" was strung out from 1913 through 1920. The haunting question is: How much material was still only in manuscript form when Stark finally gave up the ghost in 1921? And where is it now? There are rumors that there was indeed a substantial stack of ragtime masterpieces that

The Real Classics

Here is the foundation of all ragtime. These are the classics that line up ragtime with the masters of all time. Here is the genius whose spirit, though diluted and poluted, was filtered through thousands of cheap songs and vain imitations which have done much harm to the reputation of real classic ragtime.

These numbers are the American Creation and the marvel of musicians in all civilized countries.

They are NOT NEW and they NEVER will be OLD. The oftener they are heard the better they are liked.

RAGS

Maple Leaf Rag
Entertainer Rag
Sunflower Slow Drag
Frog Legs Rag
Ethiopia Rag
Cataract Rag
Easy Winners Rag
Ragtime Betty

Sunburst Rag
Ragtime Nightingale
Peacherine Rag
Cascades Rag
Elite Syncopations
Grace and Beauty Rag
Hilarity Rag

Excelsior Rag
American Beauty Rag
Nonpariel Rag
Ophelia Rag
Ragtime Dance
Climax Rag
Ragtime Oriole

WILIGHT   Meditation..E. J. Stark
FORGOTTEN   Reverie..Minor M. York
CLARICE   Waltzes..McNair Ilgenfritz
CYNTHIA   Waltzes..McNair Ilgenfritz

SONGS THAT LIVE

A PLACE IN THY MEMORY..F. W. Westhoff
A CITY FAR AWAY..Luther Adams
IT TAKES ME BACK TO THE OLD FOLKS AT HOME................Wm. Johnson
OLD MAN, YOUR HAIR IS TURNING GRAY................From the Vital Question
LOVE IS THE LIFE..Jack Steele

From Alleghenny's craggy head
The thunders crash the lightning sped,
And 'round this world the wireless spread,
And this what the message said,

"There's only one classic rag house."

Typical John Stark advertisement from the back cover of sheet music

are now lost to the world because no one considered them worth saving after Stark died. But leave us not shed a tear over what might have been, before we explore a few more treats that are still available to us from the Stark library.

Indianapolis provided the catalogue with two major additions, J. Russell Robinson and Paul Pratt, both white men. Robinson, who was a pianist for the Original Dixieland Jazz Band, composed a number of rags that seem to lend themselves to jazz treatment. His most popular number, "That Eccentric Rag," has in fact become a Dixieland standard that was performed by Red Nichols and Tony Parenti in later years.

Paul Pratt's compositions, on the other hand, are thoroughly within the classic-rag idiom. Such syncopated gems as "Hot House Rag" and "Springtime Rag" reveal a special delight in their surprising chord progressions and internal harmonies.

Pratt also had a connection with the Indianapolis publisher J. H. Aufderheide, who had previously brought out several popular rags by his daughter, May Aufderheide, among these "Dusty Rag" of 1908 and "The Thriller" from 1909, which were apparently favorites among bands in New Orleans. When pioneer jazz cornetist "Bunk" Johnson came out of retirement in the forties, he recorded both these Aufderheide rags.

New Orleans itself was the scene of a great deal of music publication throughout the ragtime era, and as might be expected, there was an exceedingly wide range of styles contained in the works. I'd like to call attention to one piece that is particularly illustrative of this: the "Triangle Jazz Blues" by Irwin P. LeClere, who is at the time of this writing still living in New Orleans. This remarkable number, published in 1917 by the Triangle Publishing Company and arranged by Joseph Martinez, is, strictly speaking, neither blues nor jazz. It is a rag, but a rag with the same St. Louis/New York/New Orleans combination of ragtime, stride, and jazz influences that make the Matthews rags so formidable. Yet it is quite distinct from any of the St. Louis rags and is actually one of the most original and carefully conceived pieces of ragtime piano arranging I've ever come across.

Of all the musical centers in the Midwest, Chicago was probably the most active and diverse. As ragtime scholar David Jasen told me, "If you come up with a rag that doesn't seem to fit stylistically in any particular camp—chances are very good that it came from Chicago!" As the industrial focal point of the Midwest, Chicago attracted a great deal of talent and consequently produced a large volume of published music. Among the numerous musicians who did significant work in the city are Tony Jackson and Jelly Roll Morton, from New Orleans; Louis Chauvin, Scott Joplin, and Arthur Marshall, from St. Louis; and New York's big

Fanny Brice's 1910 hit—her first

ragtime star, Ben Harney, whose *Ragtime Instructor*, which appeared in 1897, was actually a Chicago publication put together by Theodore Northrup.

It would be nearly impossible for me to name or analyze all the worthy rags and composers from the windy city, but I would like to mention one, and that is Joe Jordan. It is somewhat hard to associate him with any one city, as his long career took him to all parts of the world, but in 1904 he emerged from the ranks of St.

Louis ticklers and became the director of Chicago's famous Negro musical showcase, the Pekin Theater. And it was during his stay there that he produced most of his instrumental rags, including the charming "Pekin Rag."

Jordan, who was an extremely adept musical arranger as well as composer, has a long list of credits. In 1905 he helped James Reese Europe organize and direct a group called The Memphis Students, which became the first all-Negro ragtime orchestra to play in New York. Later he became associated with Florenz Ziegfeld, for whose shows he composed several hit tunes. His success was not without frustration: His song "Lovie Joe" made Fannie Brice an overnight success when she first sang it in the *Ziegfeld Follies* of 1910; but Jordan wept as he listened from outside the theater to the thunderous applause for the song's first performance—as a Negro he had not been permitted to enter the theater.

In 1917 Jordan's number "That Teasin' Rag" was taken note for note by the Original Dixieland Jazz Band as part of their big hit, "The Original Dixieland One-Step," without credit or compensation to the author. This might also have been a tragedy for him —but he won a major lawsuit against the band and was awarded a large financial settlement, one of several fortunes that he made and lost during his lifetime.

Joe Jordan died in 1971 at the age of eighty-nine, but fortunately he also appears, as do Charlie Thompson and Eubie Blake, on the *Golden Reunion in Ragtime* album, recorded in 1963. And he is well represented on an album (see Discography) released by the Ragtime Society, with his pupil, Lois Delano, playing his rags and songs.

Jordan's music is richly inventive. His songs fall into uniquely logical but often asymmetrical patterns. And it might be added, he beat out Dave Brubeck by fifty years with his number "Half and Half," written in 5/4 time in 1915.

There are a few composers who had at least one foot in the folk-rag tradition of the Midwest but concentrated their efforts in the commercial music industry of Tin Pan Alley. One of these was George Botsford, from Sioux City, Iowa, who scored hits with such rags as "Black and White Rag" as well as songs like "Sailing Down the Chesapeake Bay" and "The Grizzly Bear," which had words by Irving Berlin. Another such composer was Percy Wen-

Sheet music cover for music by Henry Lodge, a good Tin Pan Alley
writer

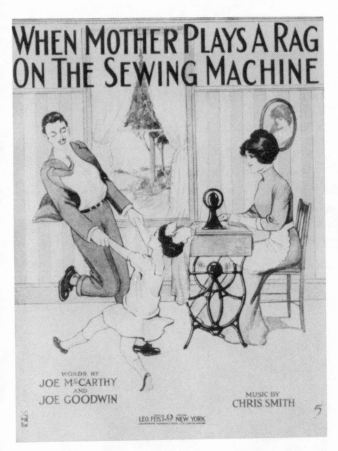

Sheet music cover for 1912 rag. Photograph by Charles Klamkin. From *Old Sheet Music*, by Marian Klamkin (New York: Hawthorn Books, 1975).

rich, who as a child soaked up the music at the magnificent House of Lords sporting house in Joplin, Missouri, then turned his folk knowledge into gold in Tin Pan Alley. He is remembered for such raggy songs as "Put On Your Old Gray Bonnet," "When You Wore a Tulip," "The Red Rose Rag" (a favorite of George Burns), and a collection of simple yet tuneful instrumental rags.

Tin Pan Alley also employed several successful Negro writers who were able to draw on their southern folk roots for inspiration. Chris Smith, who had worked his way to New York from South Carolina by way of a medicine show, wrote as many as thirteen top hits in a year. He was only able to play piano in one key (A♭), but his songs, especially the verses, have some of the most unusual and fascinating chord changes that ever came out of the Alley. His tunes like "Ballin' the Jack" and "Down in Honky-Tonk

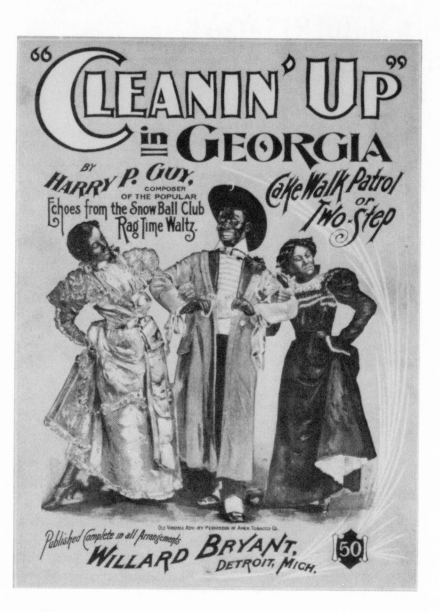

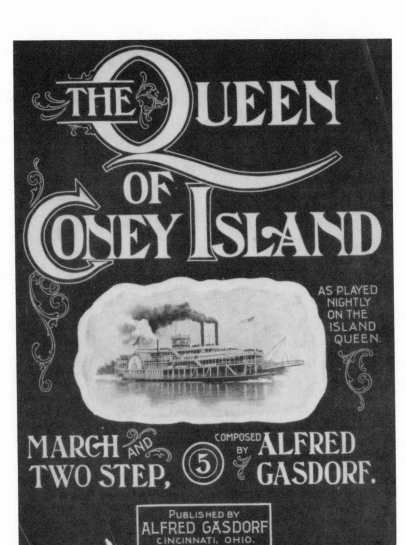

Town" would give any but the best "ear players" fits trying to figure out the progressions.

We are now down to the last few historic figures that I'd hoped to cover from the ragtime era—and I've run out of ways to really categorize them. So what follows is a somewhat random selection of composers.

Looking back to the earliest days of ragtime, there was a goodly amount of high-class ragtime that came out of Detroit, where Theodore Finney's orchestra, a Negro organization, had a monopoly on the gigs in the area before 1900. Fred Stone, who directed the group after Finney's death, wrote a couple of good rags including "Ma Ragtime Baby," and his colleague, Harry P. Guy, contributed the first ragtime waltz, "Echoes from the Snowball Club."

The Ohio River Valley, with its rich folk heritage, produced a great deal of ragtime action. In Cincinnati there were several ragtime composers who played calliope on the great steamboat the *Island Queen*. Floyd Willis's "Queen Rag," from 1911, and Alfred Gasdorf's "The Queen of Coney Island," dated 1914, both celebrate the boat's activities. Homer Denney, a third member of the group, is probably best remembered for his unique rag "Chimes," published in 1910.

This list could go on, but I hesitate to extend it much further because of the danger of producing a meaningless roster of names and dates. I would refer the serious rag researcher to the work done by dedicated ragtime historians such as Trebor Tichenor, who has edited for Dover Publications a marvelous folio of obscure rags called *Ragtime Rarities*. As for me, I seem to have run out of superlatives for the rags. Perhaps, in closing, a quote from a John Stark ad is in order:

THERE IS NOTHING LIKE THIS LIST ON EARTH,
OR ANYWHERE ELSE. JUST SHUT YOUR EYES
AND GRAB, YOU CAN'T MISS A PRIZE.

7

The 1940s Revival: Ragtime as Jazz

THE WEST COAST

Save for a few dance band arrangements and occasional cartoon sound tracks, ragtime disappeared for the last part of the 1920s and 1930s, not to reemerge until the 1940s. In 1941 a group of white musicians from the San Francisco Bay area organized the Yerba Buena Jass Band under the leadership of Lu Watters, trumpeter.

Discontented with both the overarranged big bands and, at the other extreme, the unimaginative solo-after-solo small groups that had come to represent jazz music during the swing era of the 1930s, Watters and his cohorts began experimenting with the older ensemble jazz styles of such New Orleans luminaries as Joe "King" Oliver, Jelly Roll Morton, and Louis Armstrong. Their efforts sparked a tremendous reawakening of interest in the old music on an international scale.

Turk Murphy was the trombonist with the Watters ensemble and to this day remains one of the most outstanding exponents of traditional jazz. He recalls the beginnings of the group:

> The Watters band was organized by members who were making fairly substantial livings in their various commercial groups in the San Francisco area at the time the band organized, but we all found that we weren't really contributing anything to music. We were just grinding it out, so to speak. We were making livings, but that would only go so far, and as far as

our own personal satisfaction goes, we didn't go anywhere. So roughly 1940 we broke away from all our commercial commitments and formed the band. The Watters band, as Lu had planned, was very well equipped to play any sort of music that would come up—popular music of the day, popular ballads, even Latin music. . . . We thought we were going to have to do this, and we thought we could gradually narrow the field down to where we were playing what we wanted to play. But as it turned out, the audience that attached itself to the Watters band had decided for us. When we'd play popular tunes, they'd shout and get off the floor and make a big noise and complain about it bitterly. So it eventually came down to the fact that we were playing nothing but jazz, which is what we wanted to play in the first place, but we thought we'd have to take much longer to arrive at this point.

Watters' repertoire of "jazz" tunes included blues, stomps, and rags, which the members felt were a part of the jazz tradition. As Watters explains:

Rags were part of the scene, and they were beautiful, and so why not include them in the repertoire of a jazz band that functions mainly with all horns (but not entirely)? Once in a while we'd throw it back into the rhythm section, to the piano, to a rag.

I don't know much about the history of rags—I have an instinctive feeling about them, I like them—but I was always curious about the fifty years before the establishment of the real history of ragtime. Whatever the cause, there was something going on in this country—hypothetically you might come back to a certain date, 1850, 1840 or whatever—there was something going on in this period. The greatest mystery of all time in the history of ragtime piano, to me, is the period before Scott Joplin. And by that I don't mean to detract from the great composers of ragtime, God forbid, but there must have been others maybe some people distinguished, but their names are not known too well. We can set the 1890s as the date for the beginnings of ragtime, but the *roots* existed before.

I heard a certain aspect of it when I was young. I was raised in San Francisco in the Richmond district, and in the early twenties there were a lot of people playing piano—sometimes bad ones, sometimes not too bad ones. They knew nothing about "King" Oliver, the history of ragtime or jazz, but they had a connection with this thing that went on before.

In the beginning Watters attempted to play the rags with full ensemble, but as pianist Wally Rose remembers:

"They never seemed to quite go off too well with the band. They were too difficult. They were clumsy on the horns and out of range and all kinds of stuff. Watters thought maybe it would be much better if the piano would play them. So it eventually ended up as piano solo with rhythm. Watters always wanted the banjo—banjo is such a penetrating instrument—and he never seemed to be able to get enough banjo. Between the banjo and the bass and the drums you got a lot going against the piano. And since ragtime is quite fleeting in sounds sometimes, all you can do is a single note, you got a lot of competition for that one note. Well, I felt I had to build them up some. I had to give them more body to come through. So I never hesitated then to change any of them. After all, we weren't just making it for a record where you could turn the piano up or whatever you wanted. We were actually performing these, and I had to cut through into the room so that they could be heard.

"The response to the rags was very good. And actually, when we made the first records with Watters, the record that caught on was the 'Black and White Rag.' That was the one that really got it going. In fact, Lester Koenig, who was involved in the project, said that the 'Black and White Rag' paid off the whole investment. It was played a great deal on the radio and it seemed to have great audience appeal. People ask for it even today.

"We really pioneered the revival of ragtime, because at that time it was the height of the swing era and everything like ragtime was going backwards in time. In those days everybody was more concerned about the last minute, the latest thing, the last word—and here we were flying in the face of that by going way back.

"I began to look up all kinds of rags that I was interested in and so did the others. If anyone ever heard of anything or talked about it, they would say, 'Gee, my mother used to play this. . . .' Or lots

Lu Watters's Dawn Club and band. The band (*left to right*): Harry Mordecai, Turk Murphy, Lu Watters, Bill Bart, Bob Scobey, Bob Helm, Wally Rose, and Dick Lammi. Photographs by Ed Lawless.

of times we knew pieces existed but we didn't know what they sounded like. For instance, you know, we had the 'Pastime Rags.' We found number five and we had to assume there were four in front of it, but where were they? We just could never locate them. Next one to show up was number three—and I think Gene Mayl gave me one, two, and four. It was really a thrill each time we discovered one of them. Or any new Joplin that we had never heard of—it was really something.

"There may have been someone else playing ragtime then, but at least we recorded it and got it known nationally—internationally for that matter—thereby getting lots of people interested and lots of people playing it. . . . It's such delightful music—it seems a shame that it was buried for so long."

During World War II the Watters band was not able to stay together, but in 1946 it was reorganized, stronger than ever, and it was this lineup that really stirred the excitement. The band featured a two-trumpet front line reminiscent of the "King" Oliver–Louis Armstrong work of the 1920s; alternating second trumpet was Bob Scobey; then filling out the front line, Turk Murphy with his growling trombone work styled after Kid Ory and Roy Palmer; and the remarkable Bob Helm played clarinet. In addition to Rose on piano, the rhythm section consisted of Bill Dart on drums, Dick Lammi on tuba, and Harry Mordecai on banjo (sometimes augmented by Clancy Hayes).

The band was overwhelming in its power. The two-beat rhythm section stomped like a chain-drive engine with Dick Lammi throwing his whole body into the splattering bass parts against the uncompromising "chunk" of the banjos and the precise "tack" of the wood blocks and choke cymbal.

The Watters band, which jazz historians credit as being the first of innumerable New Orleans revival groups,* held forth for two years at the Dawn Club in San Francisco making a number of excellent records, then moved in 1947 to a magnificent old building that became known as Hambone Kelly's. During the next three years Murphy and Scobey left the band, taking various members with them. Finally Lu himself quit in 1950 after a stroke. He came out of retirement only briefly in 1965 to play and record

* Marshall Stearns, *The Story of Jazz* (London: Oxford University Press, 1956) p. 153.

Lu Watters, 1973. Photograph by Ed Lawless.

an album called *Blues over Bodega* (see Discography) protesting
the building of an atomic plant on the San Andreas Fault. Otherwise
he has remained on his farm in Cotati, California, in seclusion
from the jazz scene.

Although ragtime was only a part of his repertoire, which concentrated on ensemble jazz, I think it important to understand
Watters's attitude about music and the kind of things his group
was trying to accomplish. What follows are excerpts from two
conversations I had with him in 1973 and 1975:

"No matter what happened before, all of us have roots. I don't
give a goddamn—Louis Armstrong had roots. Everybody had
roots. But we're not trying to give the impression that the roots
were more important than the individual artist. For example,
Louis Armstrong always bent over backwards to respect his roots,
whatever they were, but he had genius in himself. . . .

"We were accused many times of copying 'King' Oliver's band. How the fuck can you copy 'King' Oliver's band? We played some ensemble tunes and we wrote some ensemble tunes with the idea of the two-trumpet thing, and it was a challenge. And if you've never played second trumpet in one of these things, it's more of a challenge than you think. There's no precedent. If you're going to play second cornet, you've got to take off and dive in the wildest goddamn way. There couldn't be, for example, such a thing as copying the two-trumpet parts. You might capture the lead or the drive of a certain band, but you can't copy a second trumpet part—it's impossible. It's got to function wildly. . . . So we played a tune like 'Canal Street Blues'—we liked to play it. It was a two-trumpet tune written either by Oliver or Armstrong, one of the two great trumpet players, and they liked it; they liked to play together. So we come along as maybe the second band or third band, or maybe the first band to play one of these tunes since Oliver . . . and they say, 'You mothers copied 'King' Oliver! WHAT!? For what reason would they say that? Because we were the second band to play 'Canal Street Blues'? And here are ten thousand bands playing 'Lady Be Good' or 'Tea for Two' or some other fucking thing. We were not copying the Oliver band note for note, but at the same time we acknowledged all respect to them. *All*—like how we like this tune, and getting the inspiration on two trumpets, and so forth. We don't deny this part of it, but why should they attack us as a lone thing? Maybe I'm getting defensive, but I don't make any apologies to any of the fuckers. Now, if they want to accuse us of having roots, that's a different thing, but we never copied, and there is a hell of a difference. . . .

"There is a great temptation to say the kind of music my band plays is pretty simple and can be done easily, and that's true. But like all other things—like learning the instrument itself—you know it's simple, but before you're through with the goddamn thing, whether it's an instrument or a band, you're going to find out your work is cut out for you. It's nothing to learn the fingering on a cornet. Just the mastering of the instrument, that's the least of your worries.

"Many times, sometimes a guy comes out someplace and you want to discuss something, and you're discussing it, and you reach a certain point and it's a stalemate, to me. I can't explain it. . . . I can't say, 'There's something that happens in music that you don't understand.' Yet that's the real truth of the matter. And yet, when I say that, I ask myself, 'What kind of an egotistical asshole are you?' But there *is* something they don't understand—there's something about jazz. I mean, are you going to be sweet and pretty or are you going to be . . . what?

"For example, I was invited to hear a band some years ago . . . and there was something sickening about it. There was just something rotten about the music. It disgusted me. I mean it was *creepy* and *sweet*. And yet, I asked myself, am I so goddamned egotistical that I'm going to pass this great critical judgment on something somebody else does? That is a question for you. It's easy if you're young and striving and you're just starting out and you don't like something and you say, 'Fuck it.' But should I, as a former musician, have the privilege of imposing myself on them? I don't have that privilege and no fucker has that privilege, not the pope or any goddamn musician that ever existed has the privilege of putting his damper on somebody that's trying to do something. But there is something you can't explain to these people. . . . I don't maybe have an explanation for myself either, but it's something you can't say. . . . It's a certain thing . . . and it maybe is apparent to a woman. When somebody creeps up to her pussy in one way, and another one creeps up into her pussy in another way—and I am being slightly obscene, but it's the only connective that I can say about music—they creep up to jazz in a certain way, the *wrong* way, and goddamn, what better description do you know? But, you know, you don't want to kick someone in the ass unnecessarily, because if you kick 'im you might eliminate 'im . . . and if you eliminate 'im . . . well, . . . maybe he'd be better off eliminated, you know what I mean, but there's a limit to guts, and I'm not the guttiest person in the world. I tell you one thing though, the only thing I can claim for that old goddamn band— we had guts.

"I guess underneath all of this, the driving force is not whether you're making it commercially, although I'm not against that. I don't want to blame some band if they're making it commercially —or at least I'm not prejudging them on that point—but the driving force is whether they believe in what they are doing, not whether I believe in it, or any other jackass. If they believe in it, really believe in it, that is enough even if they fail. I don't really

give a goddamn whether they fail or not. . . . It might shock a lot
of purists, but I have a great respect for Harry James, the trumpet
player. And people come up to me and say, 'Listen, this guy is not
playing the same thing [as you are].' And I say to them, 'You're
full of shit. 'Cause this is a fuckin' good trumpet player!' (I don't
always swear that loosely, but sometimes you have to say it that
way.) I like him for the same reason I like Bunny Berigan. Both of
them have something I respect apart from their technical ability:
They are both the kind of guy that is on a high cliff and they'll
jump off and take a chance. I don't give a goddamn what their
style, I admire they're taking a chance. . . . Jack Teagarden, I
don't care whether you liked him or not, had an independence he
declared on the first three bars—'I'M MUTHERFUCKER JACK
TEAGARDEN'—and despite all his goddamn sins, I like him; he's
good.

"I remember when this guy brought this record over for me to
hear. This big goddamn band comes on—well organized as a
Miller perfection or a Benny Goodman perfection. You know, this
sort of scramble-ass big band. Anyway, it's not too good a big
band, and thirty-two bars go by, and then, right out of the middle
of all these flying turkey turds, there's this fucker Teagarden playing this high trombone, and he's really playing! There's no question about it: This is the Bad Man. I mean *really* the Bad Man. . . .
And I said, Holy Christ, what is this? How deaf-eared could I
have been all these past years? Here's this fucker playing—not
playing in the sense of trying to win or beat anybody down; he
was just playing that thing—and before the record was over I was
crying—it impressed me so much. I suddenly realized that yeah,
I had come along and played trumpet and fucked around with
a band and everything, but whatever good and whatever wrong
I did, I was blind. I had my eyes opened up. Not only to Teagarden but to many other things. I said, 'If you've been stupid
on that point, you better open your eyes about other things.' That
doesn't mean I know everything yet, but I at least didn't stop
at the point where I could have. Jack Teagarden was the first
warning I had about myself that I could be an ignorant, blind
fool and have a closed mind. . . . I got into a lot of trouble with
my traditional jazz friends on this. And I say what has to be
cut out is this bullshit, these little fine points between these

things, because all these people—Teagarden, Harry James, Dizzy Gillespie—all played beautifully. And even though I have my egotistical points, I was never foolish enough or egotistical enough to project myself into a class like that and consider myself a legend like they are. When you're talking about Teagarden, Armstrong, and people like that, you are talking about something very special, and you'd have to be the worst kind of a jerk to say, 'I am among them.' You'd have to be an abject liar. . . .

"The only claim I make for myself, and this is a true one—I was a tough country boy. Tough in this sense: At one time when I was playing trumpet I could start at six in the morning and play until six the next morning as far as endurance was concerned. That's what embarrassed me when we made the *Blues Over Bodega* record. I'd laid off for twelve years. I picked up the trumpet and went up into the hills and practiced a few times but not long enough. And we spent a great deal of time working with this girl, Barbara Dane, who sang pretty good. But before the evening was over, my chops were giving out, and for the first time in my life I'd started the record like a lion and ended up playing the trumpet like a fucking sheep. I couldn't make it. That's a frustrating sonofabitch. You suddenly have to adjust immediately to defend yourself, just to make it to the end of the record—that's all you're trying to do. . . .

"I was looking at some old pictures and here's picture after picture of our drummer, old Bill Dart, with a sour face. And I recalled the time I was the leader of a band and some woman or some hot-shot promoter would come up to me and say, 'Jesus Christ, what a difference it would make if that drummer would smile more often,' and I said, 'Well, you know, it wouldn't make as much difference as if he was playing bad drums. You know, he was playing pretty good rhythm.' Of course, that message never got across: that if you're smiling *falsely*, what relationship does that have to the music? It has none.

"Let's say you pick up a period when we were making it, twenty-five years ago or whatever. The same thing was at stake. People were writing in and saying, 'Jesus Christ, we like your band because it sounded like something else.' And I was young and strong and . . . my mind was still on the music. . . . I was adverse at first to adjusting to all this shit that was going on. . . . At first I threw them clear off. And I should have stayed that way—I'd be proud to say I stayed that way, but I didn't, I weakened. I became more of a . . . fuck-off; I started to be more considerate of them. I didn't give up totally—I maintained independence—but I was not as strong in the middle of the story as I was in the beginning, and I have to admit that, because at the beginning I was *really* pure. If some fucker came up and looked at me and put in a request and it was the wrong tune, I didn't insult him, but I'd say, you know, you can't get that kind of shit. . . . But later I became weaker. . . .

"There's a thing going on there, and we certainly recognize it with jazz fans; it's a way of life with them, a way of social life; they are not seriously concerned with the music. If you go to the average jam session, you've got forty admirers of Bix Beiderbecke, forty admirers of Louis Armstrong, forty admirers of Red Nichols, forty admirers of traditional jazz, and so on down the line to the boring extinction point. But I'm glad to say this: The pictures never change—the musicians from the 1930s until now, the ones that were talking their own language—and that to me is one of the beautiful things. We know when we're insincere. I mean, if you're gonna try and bullshit me, or I'm gonna bullshit you . . . I can recognize it, you can recognize it, because we're fucking musicians, we know something about it, and YOU CAN'T BULL-SHIT A MUSICIAN. And I'm not saying musicians are the brightest things on earth, either, because they're not; they're pretty hip, but they're not the brightest, myself included. But they speak something else. . . . We speak a particular language among musicians. And let's face it, when someone is playing music, he is not at the command of the public. The main command is the music, what he's doing. What the hell, he's not necessarily trying to blow the public off or make fun of the public. It's just that music comes first. And if he's smiling, okay; if he's not smiling, okay, too.

"You know, you've heard many people remark about Dick Lammi. He used to move up and down like this with his bass. They would say, Lammi is putting on a show, but he wasn't. These people would come up and say, 'You've got this fucking asshole—this act going on.' You know, we dug all that, and we'd say 'Fuck you, too.' There were so many beautiful things about that bastard, in spite of the humorous stories about him: He didn't have a vicious vein in his whole goddamn body. And I'll tell you the other thing about that sonofabitch: When the chips were down, that fucker burnt his body's energy for that band all day long. When the going was rough, he burnt himself up for the band—just for the band, not for Hambone Kelly's. And I saw that sonofabitch wrung out. We'd all worked pretty hard, the ones that were working, like Helm and myself. And these especially were the precious days when we were going down and we were not going to make it at Hambone Kelly's.

"The band was gradually reduced, so there were five of us left. We were in trouble then, and we wouldn't be in the most cheerful of moods. We played maybe five hundred different tunes at that time because we didn't want to get bored, rather than play eighty purist jazz tunes. We played 'Bye, Bye, Blackbird,' 'Dusky Stevedore,' 'You're Blasé,' 'Broken Promises,' everything. So that kept it fresh. Some of the purists used to come up and say, 'Jesus Christ, you're becoming a whore! They'd lay it right flat out at you and be in there looking me right in the eye the first time I met them. I'm not hot-headed and I'm not a brave man especially, but sometimes they pissed me off so much I'd say, 'You fucker! How can you deliver this one punch, this one line? What is your purpose?' Sometimes, if they were honest, they'd answer, you know, 'Why do you play 'Bye, Bye, Blackbird'?' (or something we're playing) and violating the pure concept of New Orleans jazz or whatever they want to call it. I say Fuck Them and I tell them that; and they say Fuck You—and I'll take that one, too—as long as we know where we are truly.

"But I'll tell you one thing: There is always that one thing that creeps up behind you sometimes; I don't care what you're doing, whether you're painting, playing music, or reading a good book. You get a feeling you'd rather not have that book ending, but it does. You don't have any control; you're the reader, not the writer."

Since those pre-fifties days Turk Murphy has continued to maintain the West Coast tradition—but with certain changes from the Watters band. Murphy has been able to arrange the old classic rags for the whole band, although pianist Pete Clute, who replaced Wally Rose in the late fifties, still performs many of them solo.

Turk and Pete, who have had their own club, Earthquake Mc-Goon's, in San Francisco since 1960, have only in the last few years come out of the red. There were many lean years when neither the musicians nor public support were available. The trad jazz-Dixieland revival that the Watters band had started all but died during the 1960s, but they stuck it out to emerge with what probably is the best band that Murphy has ever had.

Bob Helm, of the original Watters ensemble, still plays an eccentric and full clarinet, the perfect complement to Murphy's trombone. And in Leon Oakley, Turk has found a cornetist with the drive and intelligence to handle the most demanding lead work. There are no drums, Murphy preferring instead to depend on the excellent solidity of Bill Carrol on tuba and Carl Lunsford on banjo.

In 1976 the band seems to be an incredible anachronism, somehow a throwback to an age long ago. It still romps and stomps, and as both Watters and Murphy have commented to me, the

Turk Murphy's band in the early 1970s. *From left to right*: Bob Helm, Leon Oakley, Bill Carrol, Turk Murphy, Carl Lunsford, and Pete Clute. Photograph by Ed Lawless.

music—above all else—has guts; it says something of integrity and commitment. And that's hard to find these days.

Pianist Paul Lingle is another extremely important figure in the West Coast scene. He was the connecting link between the revivalists and what they were reviving, for he had actually heard such ragtime pianists as Mike Bernard and Jay Roberts, who played at the San Francisco World's Fair in 1915, and he had soaked up the music of the great jazz masters such as Jelly Roll Morton and "King" Oliver firsthand when they were playing in San Francisco.

During the twenties and thirties Lingle had been a highly respected commercial-jazz piano player whose credits included his accompaniment of Al Jolson in *The Jazz Singer*. In the late thirties, according to Lu Watters, who was working with him in a commercial band, Lingle told him during a long conversation after hearing Helm and Murphy: "They're great. When I heard them play, I felt the hairs on my neck start to rise. There's something about their gruff tones that you'll like."*

This was indeed a prophetic statement. It was only a short time later, Watters recalls, that Lingle embarked on a period of intensive musical reevaluation and practice:

> I was on a trip around 1938, and we were in Phoenix, Arizona, with Lingle, his wife, this girl singer, and myself. It was really out in the desert. Lingle was always pretty interested in rags, but about that time he examined himself. He says, "Lingle, you've been fucking off. Let's get down to the rudiments on the piano." And I'll tell you this—it's the truth—that temperature was really something, night and day. It was ninety degrees in the shade at least, and he practiced four or five hours every day in his BVDs. That sonofabitch worked his ass off. And he really improved. Not that he wasn't pretty good before. He always had his original touch, his tone. . . . Sometimes if you practice and develop your technique, you're not making a bit of advancement at all. You might say in flattering yourself, "I'm a little better. I'm a little faster on the guitar or a little quicker on this—better control of the pedal of the piano,

* Phil Elwood, "Paul Lingle Memorial Show" (KPFA—Jazz Archives, December 11, 1964, San Francisco).

and all that shit." And you can't throw that out the window exactly; but Lingle was doing something a little different than that: He was directing his attention towards himself, mainly. In other words, he had the faculty of being able to examine himself.

Most people who knew Lingle make the point that his personal life was an integral part of his music. And in the few recordings that we have of him this great emotional intensity seems to come through. A few selected comments on Lingle follow.

Turk Murphy:

> I can't tell you how influential Lingle was to all of us. And you can't really get a good idea from the records how good he was. You had to hear him in person playing in a bar. . . . He practiced Bach and Beethoven and . . . he was . . . what we look back on now as a fairly schooled musician, and he would have known all about everything . . . that he came in contact with. . . . Lingle apparently resented being associated strictly with the jazz scene, and he didn't like people who came in and just wanted to hear him play the classic rags. That's the way he started originally, but he came to have more of a liking for ragtime. I mean he played ragtime. This is what I think of as ragtime piano—the touch that Lingle would give it, that certain indefinable something that gives ordinary rags much more value. Some people play . . . a rag like it was a bunch of notes. Someone else comes along and plays a rag like you wonder why you haven't heard it before. Yet it's the same tune—just the personality of the musician goes into it—he plays shading and interpretation—something you can't write by any known musical marking or notation.
> He [Lingle] was extremely put out many, many times by the fact that when you play something very good people don't notice you, and you play something that you think is not as good and you get all the applause. . . . He'd fly into a rage. As a musician, you know, sometimes when you feel absolutely the worst, you play the best. It would seem that's all you have left in the world is a horn—that's how you feel alive. That's very much how Lingle felt, I'm sure . . . because a musician's life is not the most stable kind of existence anyway,

and you're bound to have your ups and downs—a lot of downs. . . . At the time you're down you cling to your horn or your instrument that you're playing. That's how it is. Lingle was this sort of person, so it had its effects on his performance. People who are serious about music and make it their way of life—they cling to the music for all they're worth—that's all they have. Outside of this they have a tangible nothing.*

Paul Lingle's wife, Betty:

Paul said one reason for all the mental illness in America is that there are so many out-of-tune pianos!

He'd also get very sentimental. We used to go to the animal pictures, you know, and he'd cry very hard, as I remember. *The Yearling*—everyone would turn around and look at him because he'd break out in sobs if anything happened to the poor little animals. . . . He kept the things that were wonderful about a child and also the things that . . . can be so irritating. . . . It looked like he got stopped at one point in his emotional growth. . . . He had this open mind and a curiosity. . . .

Paul, I think, if he wasn't a genius, he was a near-genius, and if he wasn't psychotic, he was almost. . . . But it seems to me we all learned a lot from him, you know, from knowing him. . . . I think we loved him . . . for what he was—as a person as well as a musician.**

Bob Helm:

Lingle was this sort: When he was playing and playing what he wanted to play—this was his whole world. . . . right around the piano. . . . Everything else was like on the outside looking in—all annoyances were gone. Lingle had a theory that when a person got old (I don't know how you judge this—I should have gone years ago) . . . they should go to a warmer climate. . . . I thought he was kidding about this, and all of a sudden he was gone—to Hawaii. That was his warmer climate.†

* Ibid.
** Ibid.
† Ibid.

Lingle moved to Hawaii in 1952, where he continued to play solo piano as he had done for a number of years. He died in 1963.

At present there are only a few of Lingle's recorded numbers available, eight recorded for the Good Time Jazz label in 1952 just before he left San Francisco, and several live recordings from barroom sessions. These last make up half the album *Vintage Piano*, volume three, on the Euphonic label (see Discography). There are a number of private recordings of his performances floating around here and there, which hopefully somebody may see fit to release. For Lingle is an extremely important figure in the history of ragtime, and his interpretations of the music were possibly the finest that have ever been done.

It would not be right to discuss the West Coast revival of ragtime without making note of Clancy Hayes. Clancy was an old vaudeville performer who was associated with the Watters/ Murphy/Scobey bands until his recent death in 1974. He has often been called the last of the minstrels and was reported to be Bing Crosby's favorite vocalist.

I had a chance to hear Hayes in the 1960s when he was playing intermissions for Murphy at Earthquake McGoon's. He was an extremely musical man whose deft banjo picking provided more than adequate accompaniment for his swinging vocals. And he had a fantastic repertoire that included hundreds of the best old rag songs.

He would light up if someone would request an obscure Bert Williams favorite such as "Nobody" or "If He Comes In, I'm Goin' Out," and he was able to deliver the cream of the Tin Pan Alley output with spirit and humor.

Murphy, Watters, Hayes, and the others were influential on countless younger musicians throughout the country. But most of the two-beat bands that grew up as imitations of the San Francisco style lacked the musicianship and dedication of the originators.

I personally find nothing so repulsive as the typical "straw hat," one-dimensional, "Dixieland" that so often passes for the hard-driving stuff. There have been over the years hundreds of such groups, but there have also been a few that have made lasting contributions and evolved unique styles.

One important center for trad jazz activity was, strangely enough, in Ohio, where a group of young musicians were independently starting to pick up on the older ensemble styles.

Frank Powers, a Cincinnati musician who has arranged and played clarinet for many traditional bands including my own, recalls here his own introduction to the West Coast players:

> You have to understand that when we were in high school in 1948 we were listening to the crap that everybody was listening to. Things like "How Much Is That Doggie in the Window?" and so on. So we turned to jazz. And when this revival thing happened, it was as shocking as bebop when it came out. Of course, when we first started listening, it was to people like Sidney Bechet and "Muggsy" Spanier. Then we were confronted with these West Coast records, the Watters things, and immediately the chasm appeared. We thought it was crude sounding; Lu Watters couldn't play like Armstrong; Turk sounded funny; and we figured Helm couldn't play. And we'd never heard banjo and tuba except on real old records. There were two trumpets, so we knew there must be a connection with the "King" Oliver band, but we couldn't identify the tunes—things like "Annie Street Rock." We thought, "What the hell is this?" Of course, that was an original tune by Watters or Murphy. I remember I saw a copy of the first review of the Watters record in New York. They called it corny.
>
> The thing is, none of us had any idea what they were trying to do. We had never conceived of a revival band, even though that was basically what *we* were doing. The overwhelming reaction was that nobody could believe this record had been made only two years earlier.

The most significant of the Watters-inspired groups in terms of ragtime was probably Gene Mayl's Dixieland Rhythm Kings, from Dayton, Ohio. This group played many of the classic rags, such as Joplin's "Fig Leaf Rag," plus a few rags by contemporary composers. One of Lu Watters's piano tunes, "The Villain," was arranged for band by the DRK's pianist, Robin Wettereau, into a full ensemble specialty.

Mayl has continued to operate a band through the seventies, while many of its original members have formed their own groups. For instance, Wettereau and Charlie Sonnanstine, who was the band's trombonist, went to San Francisco and formed a group called The Great Pacific Jazz Band in the 1960s, which featured several of Wettereau's band rags. One number of his, "Chelsea On Down," is an outstanding example of a rag written especially for the peculiarities of banjo/tuba ensemble.

There was one other important San Francisco phenomenon that seems to have blossomed during the 1940s revival, and that was an organization called The Gaslight Symphony Orchestra. Directed by Professor Albert White, who was an excellent symphony musician, the orchestra was an ensemble of reading players who performed many of the old stock orchestrations of the ragtime era. Although there have been several organizations of this type from time to time, White and his group seem to have captured the spirit of the music better than the others. His band was bright without being too slick, and it avoided the tendency of many studio musicians to emphasize either the "corny" aspects of the music or the pseudoclassical ones. White's records are instead robust, bouncy, and full of warmth. They display the efforts of musicians who took the music seriously enough to delve into the intellectual and emotional significance of it. The Gaslight Symphony made a couple of albums that appeared in the fifties on the San Francisco record label that are especially fine: *Your Father's Moustache*, volumes one and two (see Discography).

THE ORIGINALS

Along with the resurrection of the older forms of music that took place in the 1940s came a rediscovery of several of the original masters. In San Francisco the revivalists came across Brun Campbell, for instance, one of the old-time itinerant piano players from Joplin's early days; and during World War II, "Bunk" Johnson, an ancient trumpet player from New Orleans, made appearances with the Yerba Buena Jass Band.

When Brun Campbell was rediscovered in the forties, he had his own barber shop in California, and as Turk Murphy once told me, "You could always tell the guys who were going to see him, because of their haircuts. He wasn't really that good of a barber—but he played good ragtime."

Campbell, a white man who called himself The Ragtime Kid, had a couple of things going for him: Before 1900 he had learned the "Maple Leaf Rag" and "Original Rags" from Scott Joplin himself. But even more important, he had a clear connection with the preragtime musicians of the Midwest. His rags do not display the ingenuity and complicated structure of the classic rags of Joplin, but they do have a primitive simplicity and drive that is suggested in some of the Arthur Marshall rags and seems to hark back to an earlier time.

To my knowledge Campbell never wrote down any of his music, but he did record, and several of his numbers are available on the Euphonic label (see Discography).

Like Campbell's music, Willie "Bunk" Johnson's dates back to the last century, but Johnson reflected the styles of New Orleans jazz and ragtime as played before Louis Armstrong. Beginning around 1942 he was brought out of musical retirement, fitted with a new set of dentures, given a trumpet, and featured in several well-received concerts. And Bunk at the age of sixty-five, "still," as he said, "had what it took to stomp 'em." Remembering such standards as the "Maple Leaf Rag," he demonstrated an approach to playing that proved both exciting and especially refreshing in its contrast to the style of other New Orleans–based musicians who had continued to work throughout the years. For unlike them, Bunk's playing had not continued to evolve. When he re-emerged in the forties, his style had not been filtered through the swing era; he was a phenomenon—especially in his rhythmic conceptions—of the ragtime era.

Bunk made a bunch of recordings with older New Orleans musicians, but he said the best band he ever worked with was the Yerba Buena Jass Band. There were eight numbers recorded in 1944 (see Discography) by this group, which included, in addition to Bunk, Turk Murphy on trombone, Clancy Hayes on drums, and Bert Bales, a fine San Francisco trad jazz musician, on piano. These recordings I think are the best he ever made.

THE EAST COAST

During the 1940s the ragtime revival was also taking shape in New York, where "Bunk" Johnson began stirring up excitement in the latter half of the decade. Rudi Blesh was particularly active in those days promoting concerts and recording some of the old giants such as Eubie Blake and James P. Johnson. Blake recalls one affair in which he was on the same program with an unknown stride player from New Jersey:

> Rudi Blesh set up this Carnegie Hall concert with Willie "The Lion," Don Lambert, and me. Willie and I had never met Lambert. Now I figured the way he acted that he couldn't play the piano. He didn't have any animation and nobody ever heard of him. Of course, according to "The Lion," nobody could play the piano except "The Lion" and me. [According to Blesh, Smith initially greeted Lambert with a condescending "Hi, punk."] Well, Lambert went out there and played hell out of the piano. I told Willie, "Man, he can really play!" Willie looks down his nose and says, "He'll do." He'll do? Hell! He wiped us both off the stage!

There were also a number of youngsters picking up on the old music including several gifted piano players. In particular, Don Ewell and Dick Wellstood heard and were influenced by "Bunk" Johnson in the late forties and also absorbed the music of many of the New York stride players who were still active.

Don Ewell, although capable and willing to play the classic rags, has evolved a singular style that takes equal parts from Jelly Roll Morton and the New York players. Over the years since the forties he has made over fifty albums, recording with such diversified artists as "Bunk" Johnson, Turk Murphy, Jack Teagarden, and Willie "The Lion" Smith, but his best tracks are probably his invariably tasteful piano solos (see Discography). There's never any trickery or gratuitous flash in his performances. As one of his album covers states, "The man here just plays fine piano."

Dick Wellstood is another man of wide-ranging musical tastes and abilities. Owing to his excellent work with such groups as Bob Wilber's Bobcats, he was, for many years, considered mainly a band pianist. However, today he has started concentrating on his solo work, into which he has incorporated ragtime, among other things. One of his recent albums, *From Ragtime On*, (see Discography) covers the gamut from "Scott Joplin's New Rag" to Paul McCartney's "Yesterday." And none of these are tacky arrangements. Wellstood carefully picks his material and delivers his performances with insight and originality.

Dick gets at least one gold star from me because he was one of the first piano players since the 1920s to appreciate the music of Zez Confrey. In a characteristically independent appraisal, he decided that contrary to the prevailing "moldy fig" opinion, Confrey's music was worth recording. As he wrote in a description of "Poor Buttermilk" for the liner notes of his *Dick Wellstood Alone* album (see Discography):

> Poor Zez Confrey doesn't fit into any of the fashionable pigeonholes of "jazz." He didn't come up the river from New Orleans, didn't jam on 52nd Street, wasn't a junkie, etc. Or if he was I never heard about it. Although he composed the fabulously successful "Kitten on the Keys," he received a bare mention in Rudi Blesh's book on ragtime. I like "Poor Buttermilk" anyway. It should properly be played slowly and sweetly by a choir of drunken soprano saxophonists. This particular performance was conceived in passion and executed in rage.
>
> "Buttermilk" is a tricky piece in its original form, and I made it trickier by trading hands in the repeat of the second section, by adding additional material, etc. When I got through, I wasted so much tape trying to get a clean performance that I lost my temper and attacked the piano with the idea of destroying Confrey and his damn tune. This performance was the result. I have included it in this album because I felt the spirit of hatred more than made up for a few mistakes.*

At the height of the revival in 1947, jazz-and-ragtime historian Rudi Blesh presented a series of nationwide weekly radio programs called "This Is Jazz." Ralph Sutton, a young "Fats" Waller–influenced piano player, was introduced on one program as "the phenomenal young St. Louis pianist." The following week Blesh introduced him again, saying that it was "heartening to find so young a man—he's only twenty-four—thoroughly alive to the real artistic merit of ragtime." And on a later show Sutton was brought on as "our sensational young pianist . . . from St. Louis, which was originally the ragtime capital of the world. To say that he carries on that sort of tradition ably is really to put it mildly. . . ." Finally,

---

* Dick Wellstood, *Dick Wellstood Alone* (Columbia, S.C.: Jazzology Records, 1971), JCE–73.

in *They All Played Ragtime* Blesh and Janis acknowledge him as one of the "leaders of a whole generation of white ragtimers. . . ."

Unfortunately, Sutton himself doesn't quite see it that way: "I'm no ragtime piano player. I'm a whorehouse piano player. Whorehouse piano swings. . . . I never have liked rags or enjoyed playing them. . . . The only ragtime tunes I know are 'Dill Pickles' and 'Maple Leaf.' That's enough."*

Despite Sutton's disclaimer, he has been known to play a great deal of good ragtime—and perhaps that is the problem. He was able to sight-read a number of rags for Blesh and Janis when they were doing research for their book. He also appeared on an album of ragtime with clarinetist Tony Parenti in the forties. One of his albums of jazz piano solos was mistitled *Ragtime U.S.A.*, and in 1960 he appeared on an NBC television program called "Those Ragtime Years" with Eubie Blake and Dick Wellstood. He also recorded a few rags during the forties, such as "White Wash Man" and "The Cascades." However, in all fairness, all of his ragtime performances were in a jazz piano style, and the majority of his work is in the "Fats" Waller stride idiom. It is all clean, swinging piano playing by whatever name.

Including Sutton as a member of a ragtime coterie during the late forties seems to have been pretty much the work of Blesh and Janis, for they were researching and building interest for what would be the first book to appear on the old ragtime. If some musicians, such as Sutton, preferred not to be associated with ragtime, there would be, in a few years, a whole generation of players inspired by *They All Played Ragtime* to take up the music in earnest.

* James D. Shacter, *Piano Man: The Story of Ralph Sutton* (Chicago: Jaynar Press, 1975), pp. 100–102.

8

The 1950s Revival: Ragtime as Honky-Tonk

The traditional jazz revival that began as a revolt against the predominant commercial trends of the 1930s and 1940s came to be, more and more in the following decade, usurped by those same commercial interests. Whereas Murphy, Watters, and the rest had gone after the more profound implications of blues, stomps, and ragtime, the major thrust of most of the later revivalists was toward "straw hat" Dixieland, and ragtime was shoved under the same hat. In fact, the most popular ragtime recording of the 1940s was Pee Wee Hunt's "doo-wacka-doo" rendition of the "12th Street Rag." This Dixieland version, which came out in 1948, sold over three million copies and has been the standard version of the number ever since.

We sometimes regard the bland, "marshmallow" music of the early fifties as an indication of psychological calm on a national scale. But it was in reality a somewhat frightening period: The cold war was in full swing with its accompanying communist witch-hunts, and for the first time there was a possibility of global annihilation through atomic war. As in all such periods of stress, the popular music of the day retreated to the safe ground of escapism. And one of the more profitable musical escape routes discovered by the recording industry was through the magic door to the "good old days"—to the Gay Nineties and ragtime.

The old-time music had in the previous decade been the basis for satire in the hands of such radio favorites as Spike Jones, who featured gilded-age potboilers like "Never Hit Your Grandma with a Shovel," and Robert Q. Lewis, who resurrected such favorites as "Don't Go in the Lion's Cage Tonight, Mother Darling". But as the euphoria of the postwar days settled into the uncertain questioning of the 1950s, the music of the bygone era in one sense came to be taken more seriously: Having fun with music took on a new urgency.

When I was preparing a series for National Public Radio in the late 1960s, I conducted a small survey among a cross section of people in Columbus, Ohio, asking the question, "What is ragtime?" Not surprisingly, no one had a handy definition, but what did emerge was a connection in the minds of most interviewees between ragtime and the nostalgic embrace of anything old and a rejection of the present.

In a typical response one man said, "Ragtime to me is Laurel and Hardy, rinky-tink pianos. I sort of think of it as, like, the Gay Nineties. You know, that wild, free kind of living."

Another responded, "It's something we've done without too long—happiness!"

One woman glared at me as she vehemently declared that "ragtime music is positive. It's the positive side where people can join in and sing together rather than the folk or rock where they talk about the negative and dance apart."

Some saw it as the music, then, of the Gay Nineties, others traced it to the Roaring Twenties. A few even connected it to the music of the depression era. For everyone it was "give me that old familiar and let me pretend it's any other time but now." Please note the fundamental difference between this nostalgic appeal of ragtime and the somewhat revolutionary aspect that the West Coast revivalists had emphasized in their music. For them it was a radical departure from the blandness of the commercial music scene. They had embraced this old black music in rebellion. Ragtime was in the nature of "ass-kickin'" protest music, or at the very least a medium of personal expression. But the new ragtime of the 1950s came to represent a return to the safety of the past—and a faceless, depersonalized return at that. The new ragtime players of this era were a mythical group of back-room professors, all pictured with dangling cigarettes, flashy vests, sleeve garters, and bearing such names as Joe "Fingers" Carr, "Knuckles" O'Toole, Willie "the Rock" Knox, "Crazy Otto" . . . Who were these happy-go-lucky piano pickers who rattled off all the old favorites? Who cared?

There was in reality some fine talent behind these images, musical craftsmen of the studios who were of the same mold as the player-piano-roll artists of a few decades earlier. These men could produce damn near any kind of music that was called for, and in this era the "fun" music of the "sing-along" player-piano days became a public demand.

Most of us sophisticated, classic ragtime aficionados now turn up our noses at the corny ragtime that came out of those days, but maybe enough time has passed so that we can begin to give a fairer appraisal of the music. We'd be foolish to try to find any "heavy" messages, but there were some good points: The music was bright, well packaged, and in many cases quite original.

There were some earlier examples of the "back-room" piano style, but the first significant recordings of the genre seem to have been contained on an album put out by Capitol in the late 1940s called *Honky-Tonk Piano* (see Discography). This album includes eight ragtime selections performed by three piano players —Marvin Ash, Ray Turner, and Lou Busch—although the cover displays no mention of either the tune titles or the names of their performers. What was being sold was the image and the atmosphere. The liner notes were unsigned, but as near as I can determine, they constitute the first articulation of the happy-go-lucky conception of ragtime that was to be hammered into the public consciousness for the next twenty years:

> Breathe in deep; the air is stale, smoky and stimulating. At the far end of the room, a battered upright piano is swaying to thumping rhythm that slops beer from a half-filled glass, to drip on yellowed keys.
>
> The gal, slouching against the instrument, stares, spellbound, at the lightning dash up the keyboard, the swinging rhythm of the bass pounding out a beat as gay as pay day, as relentless as an aching heart.
>
> Who's playin? Feller named Joe. Buy him a beer, the guy's good.
>
> They called it Honky Tonk because it was the kind of music you heard in honky tonk joints in the early nineteen

hundreds. The gas-house gang loved it, and the swells, too. It was the father, or maybe the bastard son, of Ragtime.

What *kind* of music is it? You tell *us*. Hear it. *Feel* it. Pick up your glass and pound the table to it.

It's great music. The men who play it here are old timers with limber fingers and long memories. They're happy because Honky Tonk is back.

All America seems to be happy, too.*

All America was happy about the return of honky-tonk—or maybe the invention of honky-tonk. In a year or so one of the professors, Lou Busch, had launched the career of his legendary alter ego, Joe "Fingers" Carr, with the release of an original number, "Ivory Rag." He told me how it happened.

"I was an A and R man for Capitol Records, and I used to occasionally play ragtime that I heard when I was a kid. I played one chorus on a record we did with Jo Stafford and Paul Weston of 'Ragtime Cowboy Joe.' That was in 1949 or 1950. And I used to play the stuff for parties—things like the '12th Street Rag'—and it always went over. So we did the 'Ivory Rag' and 'Sam's Song' in the same honky-tonk style, and I made up the name Joe 'Fingers' Carr right there in the studio. That sold very well. In fact it was an international hit. You should have seen the records we sold in Germany and Switzerland. So I've made something like twenty-five albums of ragtime since then, and I guess you could say I've become a legend in my own time. The first two albums stayed in print for twelve years, each one.

"I was helped a great deal by Blesh's book *They All Played Ragtime* that came out about the same time. It was considered the bible on the subject. It was the best book written, but he stopped with the early black guys. He never considered the later thing that I knew as ragtime. I guess you could say I play ragtime of the twenties. I go back to the novelty players. I heard Zez Confrey in vaudeville when I was young, and I played a lot of music by those guys like Frank Banta and Roy Bargy.

"I think the first record I did was gimmicked, but I insisted on not doing that later. We had an old Crown piano in good condi-

* *Honky-Tonk Piano* (Hollywood: Capitol Records, 1950), H188.

Sheet music published in 1950 featuring photograph of Joe "Fingers" Carr

tion. We heated up the hammers and put glue on to give it a little brighter sound, but I always had it tuned to perfect pitch before the recording sessions. I believed in recording the music straight. I think they sped up Ray Turner's recording of the 'Entertainer's Rag,' and I don't know why they did because he could have played that fast himself if he'd wanted to. We never did that on my records."

Busch's success led others to enter the field. In 1954 Joe "Fingers" Carr was copied by a German piano player who recorded under the name of Otto Der Schrage (or Crazy Otto), a medley of tunes that included Carr's "Ivory Rag". This later came to be known as the Crazy Otto medley. The record had little distribution in the United States, but a note-for-note copy of it issued by Dot in 1955 became the first piano record to sell over a million copies. It made a star of Dot's ragtime artist Johnny Maddox, who took the title of Crazy Otto for his own.

Twenty years, forty albums, and eighty-seven singles later Maddox is still on the road, actively performing in nightclubs and high-class saloons. He enjoys his work as a dispenser of the good-time music, but he also makes it a point to introduce his audiences to the music of the masters of ragtime. But he says: "I have to play a little of everything. Nobody in this world can make a living playing pure ragtime. I play something people know and then they're willing to listen to something they don't know, like Joplin and Hayden's 'Sunflower Slow Drag.'"

Maddox believes that it was the sound of the gimmicked piano that sold the "Crazy Otto Medley," but on his current recording projects he is using a grand piano and doing some of the classic rags.

By the mid-fifties the saloon pianist was cropping up everywhere. TV gave us "Snarkey Parker," a Bil Baird puppet who was the visual counterpart to Joe "Fingers" Carr's music; and "Big Tiny" Little became a regular rinky-tink feature of the "Lawrence Welk Show," to be replaced by Jo Ann Castle in later years.

Nearly all the major record companies had at least one honky-tonk album in their catalogues that was sure to include most of a short list of ragtime standbys. It seemed that people could never get enough of "12th Street Rag," "Spaghetti Rag," "Dill Pickles Rag," "Black and White Rag," "Kitten on the Keys," and of course

Terry Waldo (on tuba, *far right*) and the San Francisco Red Garter Band, 1967

"Maple Leaf Rag." Lou Busch has some interesting comments on this last:

> I recorded it four times. And I'll have to say I don't really believe that Joplin wrote all of it. I know this gets a lot of the rag people mad when I say that, but the first two strains of the "Maple Leaf" are really like nothing else he ever composed. He was a melodist, and the first part of the "Maple Leaf" is a different kind of raggy thing. It was very common for guys to steal things at that time. Most of the piano players couldn't write down music, and he could. I suspect maybe it was written by somebody like Arthur Marshall. [Marshall's daughter, Mildred Steward, supports the conjecture that the "Maple Leaf" was a collaboration between Joplin and her father.]

Because if you get a hit like he did with "Maple Leaf"—what's the first thing you do? You write another one like it. He never did.

In the 1960s new establishments began popping up as sanitary, suitable-for-the-family re-creations of the honky-tonk saloons. Shakey's Pizza Parlors began serving "fun—also pizza" with rinky-tink piano and banjo accompaniment. And in a similar vein a rash of banjo bars appeared, beginning with the Red Garter chain, then followed by the Your Father's Moustache and hundreds of smaller operations. One of these good-time parlors, Mickey Finn's, was reconstructed in full on television for a season with host ragtime piano player Fred Finn.

I myself spent a number of years working in various Shakeys's and Red Garters. I still have occasional nightmares about the many hours I put in sitting at an upright on which usually three or four notes did not operate at all and the rest were hopelessly out of tune; wearing a dirty red vest, clip-on bow tie, and styrofoam straw hat; fighting off an army of small, ill-mannered children with pizza grease dripping off their fingers and cheeks; and accompanying a song slide projector* that invariably malfunctioned midway between the halves of a two-slide song. However, I must admit that in retrospect the whole thing was a learning experience. There's no substitute for time spent on the job where you have a chance to experiment. It's just too bad the whorehouses aren't hiring piano players any more.

---

* The tradition of song slides goes back to the ragtime era when the words to popular songs were projected in theaters for sing-along. Later, the movies used the "bouncing-ball" technique to guide the singers.

9
The 1960s Revival: Back to the Roots

THEY ALL PLAYED RAGTIME

In spite of the commercial deluge of ricky-tick ragtime, the seeds of interest in the classic stuff had been sown with the publication of *They All Played Ragtime** in 1950. The interest grew slowly, but by the 1960s there was a fair-sized underground group of musicians and fans who knew about ragtime and were familiar with the names of the historic musical figures who had been described in the Rudi Blesh–Harriet Janis collaboration. Blesh told me how the book happened to come about:

"The writing of *They All Played Ragtime* sort of began as a dare, really. Mrs. Harriet Janis and I had a recording company called Circle, and we were recording jazz. I had finished writing *Shining Trumpets*, which came out, if I remember, in 1946. And I wanted to be more in the production angle and the signing of older artists that had been sort of lost, left into obscurity, and trying to restore them. And the thing that really got me onto the ragtime kick were two things that happened.

"One summer Mrs. Janis said, 'You should write another book.' I said, 'I don't want to write another book, it's too much work. Besides, I have written a book on jazz; I don't really have any

* Rudi Blesh and Harriet Janis, *They All Played Ragtime* (New York: Alfred A. Knopf, 1950).

Note: Information pertaining to recordings mentioned in this and succeeding chapters may be found in the Discography.

subject that I particularly want to write on now.' She said, 'Why don't you write a book on ragtime?' I said, 'Oh, for heaven sakes, that all happened so long ago that I couldn't get enough material to write on it.' She said, 'Of course you could.' So she argued about the thing until I finally said, 'Well, look, if you're really so set on doing a book on ragtime, I'll do it if you'll do it with me. We'll make it a collaborative effort.' And the matter sort of rested there; it hadn't gone any farther.

"Then . . . in the meantime, Tony Parenti came to see Harriet because he thought she was more approachable on the thing, wanting to do a ragtime album. Instrumental ragtime. And she worked alone on this thing with him without me knowing about it until they had the thing set up into the rehearsal stage. She got me to come over one afternoon. When I walked in, they began to play and all I had to say is, Ragtime is Beautiful! It's absolutely great! It wasn't really jazz and it wasn't pure ragtime, but it was in between the two. Some beautiful clarinet going, some nice solid piano, tuba underneath. . . . And they had some nice arrangements of some usual rags: 'Sunflower Slow Drag,' 'Swipesy,' but also some unusual ones like 'The Indian Intermezzo, Hiawatha,' where Bill Davison is really hitting a lick on the thing. 'Course I said, 'We've got a recording date.'

"Then we began doing the research thing [the book]. We gave ourselves a year to do it. We got a contract to publish it, and we started with very few contacts. . . .

"Somebody in Harlem told us, 'You better go out and see Shep Edmond in Columbus, Ohio.' Well, Shep Edmond was a gold-mine. Here was a man already then, in 1949, up in his eighties; he really went back into the ragtime period. He told us how ragtime was doing, not in 1899 when Joplin wrote the 'Maple Leaf' but in 1893 at the Chicago Exposition. . . . He told us the people who were playing and the places where they played. Then he said, 'Now, if you're going on west, see so-and-so in St. Louis, and he gave us a list of people. Then when we'd get to each town, of course, we didn't know how many of these people were still alive, because we were researching a thing that had mainly happened 1899 to 1910. This is 1950, fifty years later. People we were talk-ing to were already almost ready to go. Matter of fact, on that subject, I could say that we interviewed almost an even one hundred people, and when the book came out, within one year after it was out, forty out of the hundred were dead. That's how touch-and-go this thing was.

"Anyway, we would find these people and they would lead us to others. And we had a real interesting thing along those lines: When we went to Sedalia, where, of course, so much of it happened before St. Louis, we found another goldmine in G. Tom Ireland, who was not strictly speaking a ragtime player but who was a musician of the period, black of course, clarinet player, band man, and who knew Joplin very well. And he sent us to so many people; and we wanted to find one of Joplin's pupils, Arthur Marshall, who had moved to Kansas City. And we said, 'Mr. Ireland, is Arthur Marshall still alive?' He said, 'I'm not sure, and I don't know where he lives, but you know how to find out, don't you?' We said, 'No. Do we go to Kansas City and ask people on the streets, "Do you know Arthur Marshall?" ' 'No,' he said, 'Go to the leading Negro undertaker and ask him. . . . He'll know every old man there because he's just waiting for the day that he'll be his next job.' And wasn't he ever right. We went to see this Negro undertaker in Kansas City, and when he understood that we wanted to talk about ragtime people and jazz people he said, 'Yes, I know where Mr. Marshall is.' But he says, 'You know, I'm the one who embalmed 'Fats' Waller.' And he gives us this long story about 'Fats' Waller being taken off the train, you know, dead in Kansas City and having to be lifted through the window. So then, when he'd finished this long story, he said, 'I did a beautiful job on him. He looked just like he did in life. . . . He could do anything but play.' Then he said, 'I'll take you over to Mr. Marshall's,' and he did.

"Anyway, the thing is that the only way we could get a story on ragtime in book form was to get it from the mouths of the people who played it and made it, composed it and published it, and so forth, because there had been no book written on it. Here is this music that completely changed the course of American music, and there never had been a book written on it."

Probably the first entertainer to take the message of *They All Played Ragtime* to heart and apply it to live performance was

"Ragtime" Bob Darch. He was not an older piano player who remembered ragtime from the 1920s, nor was he a commercial recording artist cashing in on a fad, and he was certainly not a jazz musician. Darch was and is, first and foremost, a lover and performer of real ragtime. And although dressed in the stereotype straw hat, red vest, and sleeve garters, he has since 1955 continued to sell the music of Joplin, Marshall, and the rest to audiences throughout the United States and Canada. While he has organized and appeared on numerous concerts, record dates, and television shows over the years, he has always been most at home on the saloon circuit, which he feels represents the mainstream and lifeline of ragtime. He says:

> It is interesting to note that most successful ragtime composers wrote their best rags while working a saloon or sporting house. . . . Why? The excitement: women, the modern language, the dangers, the curtain of smoke, etc.—all contributing in creating a mood that inspires the composer to put what he hears and sees into music and onto paper. . . . Anyone who thinks Scott Joplin was inspired to write "The Entertainer" or "The Favorite" while sitting in his parlor on a Sunday night is naïve. . . .

Darch, I think, has been underrated in terms of his contribution to the preservation of this music. For in his missionary zeal he has reactivated the careers of many ragtime pioneers like Eubie Blake and Joe Jordan, and to his credit he has also helped launch the careers of a group of younger players including Steve Spracklen and Trebor Tichenor, who have continued to spread the ragtime message.

But by far the most influential ragtime artist in the sixties was Max Morath, though, as he would be the first to say, he is not what you would call a ragtime piano player:

> Probably in the last twenty years nobody has made their living with ragtime; I certainly haven't, not by a longshot. There are one or two pianists, Bob Darch, possibly Johnny Maddox, who have made what you could call a living—that is, pay their

bills. I have made a living with the whole idea of approaching the past and reconstructing it and reperforming it, but I haven't really made a living as a ragtime pianist. I've done a lot of writing and a lot of research so that when I do ragtime I put it in a framework. Like the current show that I'm doing right now, which I've been doing for three years now. It's a theatrical package—runs two hours. But there is no more than about fifteen minutes elapsed time of ragtime piano playing in it. Really, only about twelve minutes. The rest of it is humor, history, satire, monologue, songs, connectives, all kinds of things that have to do with a lot of other disciplines besides the piano. It's more the theatrical discipline, the idea of entertaining, with a kind of educational subfunction. If anybody asks me what I do for a living, I say, "I mess with Americana."

Max first came to national attention in 1960 with a marvelous series he did for educational television called *The Ragtime Era*. In it, and in a following series called *The Turn of the Century*, he presented a comprehensive, highly entertaining exploration of the music and its context in American life.

Morath's next major triumph came in 1963, when he opened at the Blue Angel in New York with a delightful ragtime quartet.

Morath:

"I had been working for several years on various ideas on how to broaden the essential pianistic sound of classic ragtime; that is, to open the performing of the music up to instrumentalists on other instruments and still be fairly faithful to what the composers intended in my estimation. I've experimented with large orchestras and using modern orchestrations, also period orchestrations. And in the mid-sixties I had a group called the Original Rag Quartet on tour for a while, and it was with this group that I got into this idea of using fretted instruments to expand the ragtime sound. Mandolin, banjo (both five-string and tenor), acoustic guitar, and string bass. . . . And I think this is justified for several reasons: Those instruments were very much a part of the turn-of-the-century scene, and they were used for this music when it first came along, with the piano still at the center, of course. Also, these instruments have a kind of a percussive quality which lends itself to the ragtime sound. And the third reason, and it may be a little bit self-serving, is that these are the instruments that the people of America, particularly the young people, are playing today. So if there is to really be a regeneration, a great renewal of interest in the performing of ragtime, it is going to be on these instruments. That's one direction I've gone with it. . . . I'd like to see some young groups come along and take a sound like this and expand it and run with it. Even if they go electric with it. I'd like to do that myself. If I had the time, I'd love to do an album of electric ragtime. One of the sounds I'd like to experiment with is the electric harpsicord, along with electric mandolin, electric guitar and string bass, electric bass—it'd be a great sound."

Max has indeed been a tireless experimenter but also a very savvy communicator. He has done television, radio (many years with Arthur Godfrey), Broadway, nightclubs, records—all of consistently high quality and geared for the needs of the particular medium. All in all, ragtime music could have no finer public spokesman.

Morath's idea of playing ragtime on string instruments was actually picked up by a few other groups who were in the main interested in jug-band music. Sam Charters and folk singer Dave Van Ronk put together a group in the 1960s called The Ragtime Jug Stompers that played, among other things, several classic rags using the instrumentation of guitar, banjo, mandolin, jug, thump-tub, and washboard. This harks back to the early jug bands such as the Dixieland Jug Blowers, who recorded ragtime numbers such as "House Rent Rag" and "Banjorino" during the 1920s.

Renewed interest in ragtime brought about a few related television programs in the early 1960s, but as is the custom in the United States, home of disposable culture, it is now impossible to see them. In the case of Max Morath's NET programs, the videotape copies have been erased because contractual rights to the music only lasted for ten years. The only other significant television program was a special called "Those Ragtime Years," produced by NBC for its *Project Twenty* series in 1960. This excellent documentary–variety show integrated old films and stills from the ragtime era with performances by Hoagy Carmichael, Dick Wellstood, Ralph Sutton, Eubie Blake, Dorothy Lauden, and the Wilbur de Paris band. Unfortunately, the show was involved in a lawsuit over the use of certain material from Blesh and Janis's *They All Played Ragtime*, and consequently the show was only aired once. The videotape has long since been erased.

Max Morath

In the music-publishing field the story was equally depressing. Previous to the sixties there had been only one folio of published ragtime available: A dozen or so rags were printed in an album by the Melrose publishing company, which had inherited the Stark catalogue. Max Morath effected the publication of *One Hundred Ragtime Classics*, which appeared in 1963; but by and large the major publishers showed not the slightest interest in issuing the old music. There was one single exception: Mills Music began publishing ragtime owing largely to the efforts of one Bernie Kalban; and if anyone has carried on the tradition of John Stark in his devotion to the publication of rags, it has been he. While at Mills, Kalban was responsible for the publication of two excellent folios containing some of the best of Joplin, James P. Johnson, and others; he followed this with *The Golden Treasury of Ragtime* (1964), which consisted of thirteen previously unpublished Joseph Lamb rags. Kalban has continued quietly to plug for ragtime at E. B. Marks Music, through which he has managed to bring about the publication of both *Max Morath's Giants of Ragtime* (1971) and the more recent *Sincerely, Eubie Blake* folio (1976). Kalban is one of the few people in the publishing field who really gives a damn about the music.

THE RAGTIME PEOPLE

In the sixties, spearheaded by a few key individuals such as Darch and Morath, there began to appear what you might call a ragtime fraternity. These people collected music, piano rolls, what few records were available, and at least on the surface longed for the day when America would come to recognize its grand ragtime heritage.

Although almost everyone in these circles quoted from the wealth of information contained in *They All Played Ragtime*, it was still very hard to actually hear the music. So what developed was a small network of organizations and individuals who kept in contact by way of periodic get-togethers. It was often possible at that time to attend one of these soirées and meet personally with nearly everyone who was actively involved in the preservation and rediscovery of ragtime.

Probably the most successful and long running of these affairs has been the St. Louis Ragtime Festival held every summer on the magnificent *Goldenrod Showboat*. Begun in 1965 as a one-day gathering of piano players, it has gradually become an annual event lasting a full week. Although it has been described as "the Woodstock for geriatrics," it actually draws quite a cross section of people and over the years has featured nearly every major ragtime and traditional jazz performer in the country.

The focus of the festival has at times been more on traditional jazz and Dixieland than on ragtime, but the promoters have worked to maintain a balance and give every artist a chance to perform in a good atmosphere. There have always been at least five locations of musical activity on or near the boat, with continuous entertainment and at least one after-hours free-for-all, usually held on the levee, with literally hundreds of musicians, professional and amateur alike, jamming until the sun breaks through.

The hosts of the St. Louis festival have always been The St. Louis Ragtimers, who have been performing rags, stomps, and blues on the *Goldenrod Showboat* for well over a decade. This group, which has changed personnel slightly from time to time, always includes Trebor Tichenor on piano, Al Stricker on banjo and vocals, and Don Franz on tuba. Although they do some jazz numbers and blues, it is the folk ragtime and rag songs that are their forte. Trebor's piano specialties, like "Black Mountain Rag" and Brun Campbell's "Lulu White," bounce along with that down-home Missouri ragtime flavor. And Al Stricker maintains a large repertoire of old "sportin'-house" tunes that retain the humor and spirit of the ragtime era. I believe the Ragtimers also have the distinction of being the first group in fifty years to record "When Ragtime Rosie Ragged the Rosary."

There were two ragtime publications started in the sixties that are still around today, and both have had live performance as part of their operations. Since the mid-sixties the Maple Leaf Club of California has had monthly meetings that have featured a variety of talent from the Los Angeles area and guest artists from all over the country. Over the years the programs have included the old-timers of the business, such as Eubie Blake, Joe Jordan, and Shelton Brooks, as well as younger players such as Bob Long, Jim Hession, Dave Bourne, and Bill Mitchell. Dick Zimmerman, who recently did a recording of the complete works of Scott Joplin for Murray Hill, has organized the events and also cranks out the usually informative house organ of the club, *The Rag Times*. Information about the Maple Leaf Club and the *Rag Times* can be obtained by writing to the Maple Leaf Club, 5560 West 62nd Street, Los Angeles, California 90065.

Another major ragtime organization to emerge in the sixties is the Canada-based Ragtime Society. Like The Maple Leaf Club, the Society began publishing a monthly periodical, *The Ragtimer*, with various sorts of information on ragtime, but it has also engaged in the extensive effort to record various new performers and composers. Their address is P.O. Box 520, Weston, Ontario, Canada, M9N 3N3.

In 1963 the society produced an album entitled *Classic and Modern Rags* by Tom Shea. One side was devoted to classic rags, which was welcome enough, but the other side contained six delightful original compositions by Shea in the classic-ragtime tradition. In the next few years the society followed up with a series of albums devoted to classic ragtime and its related branches. Through these, the music-hungry fans became acquainted with a diverse range of young players, from John Arpin, who plays a clean, sophisticated, cosmopolitan style, to a stomping, down-home Charlie Rasch.

The society has also hosted a yearly "bash" in Toronto, which, unlike the St. Louis festival, presents, under the expert guidance of rag picker Tex Wyndham, a varied and entertaining program of piano ragtime.

THE NEW RAGTIMERS

In this section I would like to call attention to some of the outstanding performers of the 1960s; they have been by and large overlooked by the revival of the 1970s, which is too bad, because in many ways their playing, especially in terms of warmth and feeling, surpasses anything that has come along since.

One of the most impressive piano players I've ever heard is Bob Wright from Chicago. I started hearing rumors of Wright's abilities around 1964 from Trebor Tichenor and was frankly skeptical of the claims that Trebor made for him. For instance, Wright was supposed to have a repertoire of at least five hundred rags that he could play from memory and a technique that encompassed every style from primitive Missouri ragtime to Thelonious Monk. This all turned out to be true! Wright, equipped with perfect pitch and a steel-trap mind, was able to play anything. (I say "was" because it has been his custom to play in one bag for a while and then drop it entirely for something else. This has often been accompanied by startling and complete changes in his appearance—first long hair, then shaved head, beard, etc.)

The first time I met Bob at one of the St. Louis festivals, he was in his "know-every-song-from-memory" period. This included nearly every number listed in *They All Played Ragtime* and more. I sat in his living room not long after and went through the book picking out numbers at random. A classic rag would be performed in the carefully conceived Joplin piano-roll style—then he would shift gears and swing into a terrifyingly complex Luckey Roberts stride piece like "Nothin'," then an obscure, unpublished Joe Lamb rag like "Rapid Transit." The sheer volume of his repertoire was astounding enough, but Wright captured every musical nuance as well. If the tune came from a record, he would imitate the record; if it was a piano roll, he could duplicate the strange, jangling qualities of the perforated recording even down to the mistakes. But his most incredible accomplishment, in my opinion, was the synthesis of styles: he was fond of taking a popular tune like "Goldfinger" and turning it into a complicated stride vehicle or doing one of Scott Joplin's rags in ¾ time.

In addition to all this, Wright was also the master of style reconstruction: He could take a number that James P. Johnson had recorded late in his life and play it the way Johnson might have when he was in his prime in 1917. Wright did Ben Harney's "Cakewalk in the Sky" as a stride number on the basis of the description of Harney's playing style rather than using his greatly simplified published work.

When I first met Wright he had already dropped his Jelly Roll Morton tunes. And by 1970 he was no longer doing most of the classic and stride rags and had begun concentrating on the novelty rags. These he had discovered were the "most pianistic" of the ragtime styles, and with his characteristically total commitment, he had learned hundreds of the Zez Confrey and Roy Bargy numbers from rolls, sheet music, and records.

At the St. Louis Ragtime Festival in 1974 Wright was immersed in the music of the piano-roll wizards such as Felix Arndt and Phil Ohman. It had been believed that their piano rolls had been made by multiple playing to get the three-hand effect and that it was impossible for one person to play them note for note in live performance. Bob was busy disproving this theory. (I *still* have my suspicions that he may be the first person ever to accomplish this feat.)

Unfortunately, Wright's incredible musical proficiency has been afforded little public exposure. He has not recorded over the years except on low-quality home recorders from time to time. There is one recording of his work made in 1974 by Dirty Shame Records scheduled for release, but at the time of this writing it has not appeared on the market.

Wright was not the only one to play all of the known classic rags. There were recordings made of all the Joplin rags and parts of the opera *Treemonisha* well before the 1970s. To "Knocky" Parker goes the credit for the first complete recordings of the Joplin rags (except for one rag, the "Silver Swan," which was not known at that time) and also the complete works of James Scott, both issued in two-record sets by Audiophile. This was a pretty amazing feat, especially considering that Parker doesn't read music. He has also recorded a five-record volume of Jelly Roll Morton tunes and was in the process of doing the works of Joe Lamb the last time I checked.

Parker actually has two styles of playing. In live performance he is, in purely physical terms, terrifyingly strong; he threatens to destroy the piano. But in recording sessions he seems to become rather subdued, even to the extent of performing some of the rags most delicately on celeste and harpsichord. Interestingly, Charlie Thompson once said that some of Parker's recordings sound like Louis Chauvin in that both of them were fond of adding tenths to the left hand and introducing advanced harmonics.

The first recordings of *Treemonisha* were organized by Sam and

Ann Charters in the late fifties. They devoted one side of an album to selections from the opera as performed by Ted Puffer and the Utah State University Choir, and the other side to Joplin piano works as executed by Ann Charters.

There have been a number of piano players, such as Dick Well-stood, Don Ewell, Bob Wright, and Paul Lingle, who have been greatly influenced in their own styles by that of Jelly Roll Morton, but none of them have been so exclusively involved as Butch Thompson and Bob Greene, both of whom could be classed as Jelly Roll players.

I would have to consider Thompson, who plays clarinet with the Hall Brothers Jazz Band in Mendota, Minnesota, one of the most purely musical piano players to show up at the festivals. It's always amazing to me that he can follow a full seven-piece band on stage and hold the audience; I've always had to resort to sing-ing or some form of theatrical bullshit to get the crowd—Butch just plays.

Bob Greene used to attend the festivals a great deal but has more recently been involved in re-creating not only the solo work of Jelly but also the band material. Lately he has won critical acclaim for his concert show, in which he plays, conducts, and narrates the story of the legendary New Orleans jazz master.

Perhaps a third musician, Jim Dapogny, should be included in this section. Although Dapogny has been playing in the Jelly Roll fashion since the mid-fifties, only recently has he made any commercial recordings. Of late he has been involved with the mammoth project of transcribing all of Morton's piano solos for publication by the Smithsonian Institution.

There are a couple of entertainers who have been especially effective in combining their musicianship with their research, and I would like to cite them here. David Jasen's playing reflects the work he has done in the last decade or so in analyzing and cata-loguing the recorded output of the ragtime era. He has dug up such unusual gems as Zez Confrey's "Nickel in the Slot," in which he imitates a faulty nickelodeon; Mike Montgomery has likewise utilized his extensive knowledge of piano rolls in his piano play-ing: Mike can play the verse and chorus of damn near any tune that was ever cut into a perforated roll.

There were a few jazz pianists who made the ragtime scene, including Bill Taylor and Hank Jones. Jones made a nice album for ABC called *This Is Ragtime Now* on which he interpreted many of the Joplin works, carefully but with a fine, swinging feel. More recently he did several tracks on Max Morath's album of Irving Berlin tunes for Vanguard.

Dick Hyman is another New York jazz musician who, like Jones, has done some ragtime as part of his regular work as a studio musician. He was one of the piano players to assume the roles of "Knuckles" O'Toole and Willie "the Rock" Knox for Grand Award Records in the early 1960s. Hyman, like many piano players at the time, did not want to be labeled as a ragtime musician. But he nevertheless played very well in the context of honky-tonk piano, even contributing a couple of his own compositions. In the 1970s Hyman has recorded many of the stride pieces of which he is apparently proud enough to release under his own name, and in 1975 he did the complete works of Scott Joplin for Victor.

The ragtime revival was not limited to the North American continent by any means. There were also some great recordings that came out of Europe, especially England, where a trad jazz boom in the fifties produced a flood of band ragtime.

One of the best ragtime albums of all time was made by the English jazz trombonist Chris Barber in the fifties. It was called *Elite Syncopations* and featured band· versions of many of the numbers from Stark's *Red Back Book of Rags*. However, the most interesting tunes on the album were several rags that Barber recorded as trombone trios and quartets. Using tape overdubbing to play all the parts himself, Barber's virtuoso performances, thoroughly within the spirit of the ragtime tradition, come off as masterpieces.

The English trad jazz scene also produced ragtime recordings by Ken Colyer, Acker Bilk (remember "Stranger on the Shore"?), Kenny Ball (remember "Midnight in Moscow"?), and a group of mad Englishmen called The Temperance Seven, who recorded Scott Joplin's ragtime waltz, "Pleasant Moments," under the pseudonym The Unnatural Sextet. Ragtime was in fact a part of the repertoires of most of the English trad groups, and there was an enormous number of them.

There were also a few piano players from Great Britain whose records gained them reputations on this side of the ocean: Neville Dickie, who played ragtime for the BBC, has produced several good albums. And Ian Whitcomb, who enjoyed some fame with his hit rock-and-roll single in 1965 called "You Turn Me On," has spent a great deal of time in the States researching the early music of Tin Pan Alley, which he performs with piano or ukelele accompaniment.

I must apologize for the many omissions in this discussion, but I believe the point has been made clearly: There were a number of excellent musicians playing ragtime well before the world "discovered" Scott Joplin in the 1970s.

10
The 1970s:
The Joplin Revival

THE CLASSIC JOPLIN

The 1960s had witnessed a reawakening of interest in classic rag-time pretty much as it had been described in *They All Played Ragtime*, but this had been a small-scale phenomenon. The rag-time bag was still somewhat esoteric and ill defined. Most of the musical intelligentsia, whether jazz or classical oriented, still viewed ragtime as a primitive form of jazz at best, and your aver-age "guy on the street" simply had had no real contact with it. And how could he? As ragtime hadn't yet been pigeonholed and marketed, it had no real identity. To get air play, music must first fit into a category—appeal to some specific audience. By the six-ties we had moved into the age of audience analysis and formula radio. Ragtime simply didn't fit into any of the customary cate-gories. It was not rock, middle-of-the-road, easy listening, country and western, classical, jazz, or soul. Finally a chink appeared in one of the markets. In 1970 the classical-music buffs discovered the music of Scott Joplin. This is how it came to be.

The story begins with William Bolcom, a gifted young com-poser with impressive, legitimate credentials (studied at the Paris Conservatoire, doctor of musical arts from Stanford, etc.) who came across Joplin by accident in 1966. While meeting with Nor-man Lloyd of the Rockefeller Foundation for the purpose of obtaining a grant, he learned of the opera *Treemonisha*. Bolcom's interest was piqued, and so he was directed by Lloyd to Rudi

Blesh. Rudi got him a copy of *Treemonisha* that the Ragtime Society had published a few years before, and put Bolcom in touch with Max Morath. From Morath, Bolcom obtained a number of Xerox copies of some of the rags, and then he was hooked. Bolcom:

> I was trained as a classical musician all my life, but I was always interested in popular music. According to my teachers it wasn't as good, but I loved it anyway. I just didn't have enough nerve to tell myself to go ahead and play it seriously, but I loved it. . . . When I was at the Paris Conservatoire I won the second prize instead of the first prize for a string quartet because I stuck a tune something like "Rock-a My Soul in the Bosom of Abraham" in the last movement. When I discovered ragtime, I discovered a kind of music that I could relate to in every way. I got knocked out by Scott Joplin. I think he's one of the great guys of all time. He interested me because he was the first American who was able to take all of these various sources of music and synthesize them. . . . That's what I want to do in music, too; I want to put all my musical experiences into one personality. I'm not a ragtimer; I'm not interested in spending the rest of my life going to ragtime festivals and trading old sheet music; I'm not interested in antiques. I'm more interested in things that are new for me. I notice the tendency among a lot of ragtime people to say it's good because it's old. I say if it's old and beautiful, fine; if it's *new* and beautiful, equally fine. I'm not interested in Joplin simply because he was black, either. It's the music itself that counts. I'm not really a ragtime fan. I like some of these other composers—Lamb, Scott, and Artie Matthews—but none of them are as good as Joplin.

Bolcom's enthusiasm for Joplin led him to set the wheels in motion for several related projects: He sent the scores of *Treemonisha* to a black composer friend of his, T. J. Anderson, who was then teaching music in Tennessee. Anderson immediately began to orchestrate it and make plans for an all-black performance of the work. More on that later.

Bolcom also contacted Vera Brodsky Lawrence, who had recently edited and arranged for publication the collected works of Louis Moreau Gottschalk. She had just received a grant to edit, for the New York Public Library, an Americana-collection music series, and Bolcom convinced her that the Joplin works would be a logical starting point for the project.

In the meantime Bill had also aroused the interest of some of his friends in playing and composing rags. He and William Albright set to work writing brilliant modern rags for their own amazement and amusement. Albright produced a "Grand Sonata in Ragtime," and Bolcom himself came up with a large body of original ragtime compositions, many of which he later recorded.

Another of Bolcom's friends who became interested in Joplin was Joshua Rifkin. It was Rifkin who would in a few years record an album of Scott Joplin rags in a careful and precise classical style that would elevate Joplin to the ranks of respected classical composers.

Rifkin is basically a conservatory-oriented piano player with music degrees from Juilliard and Princeton, but he has been interested in jazz and ragtime since he was a child. I talked with him in the spring of 1975:

"I was first aware of Scott Joplin, actually, when I was about ten years old—I was very interested in New Orleans jazz. My brother and I used to go downtown in New York where the older jazzmen from New York, Chicago, and New Orleans were still playing. And I met them, played with them, and talked with them a great deal. I got to know particularly Clarence Williams, the old song writer and pianist. And so among my experiences I came across some of the Scott Joplin rags. I heard Bunk Johnson's recording of 'The Entertainer' and I played the 'Maple Leaf Rag,' as any jazz pianist had to. Of course, I played it like a jazz pianist—I played *my* 'Maple Leaf Rag.' My whole view of ragtime was the conventional one for the time. Ragtime was part of early jazz. Then I drifted out of it for a long time.

"Around 1968 or so Eric Salzman, a composer and critic in New York who was a very good friend of mine, mentioned to me some rags that he had gotten from Bill Bolcom, who was a good friend of both of ours from other connections, and said he was tremendously taken with the stuff. My first response was that I thought I had known ragtime from my jazz days, but when I started looking at it I discovered that it was something completely different from what I had taken it to be. I began playing the stuff endlessly . . . but just for myself and friends. Then occasionally we would have a ragtime-and-early-jazz evening on WBAI radio. Bill and I and a couple other people would play. There was a kind of burgeoning interest in all of this music.

"Now, at this time I had changed my style and developed, I suppose, the somewhat controversial approach to ragtime I have now. In my view much of ragtime—not all of it but certainly Joplin's—was a very classical music. It was not meant to be played the way people conventionally played it—the way I myself had played it in my jazz days. I came to see that it should be played *as written*, and that's what I did.

"I am not, as many people think, simply a person from the classical field who decided that there was something exotic here in ragtime and played it this way just because I didn't know better and could play no other way. It was a conscious decision on my part to do it this way. I felt at one point that I would like to see this music recorded, and since I felt that it was basically classical music, I felt it should be on a classical label. Luckily, I had one more or less at my disposal—Nonesuch Records. I had a longstanding association with them and considerable freedom as a recording artist and producer to make records that interested me.

"Actually, my first fascination was with Lamb, but then I figured if I recorded any ragtime, it should really be Joplin simply because, by all common consent, he was the central figure. As it happened, of course, the more I played Joplin the more I became interested for musical reasons as well. Indeed, Joplin holds up, I feel by far the best of the lot.

At any event, I spoke to Nonesuch about the project, I guess in the spring of 1970, and everybody was enthusiastic about it. We guessed, of course, considering the success that WBAI had had with ragtime, that we would sell a few more albums than with the Renaissance music I usually recorded. But I really mean a *few* more albums: We were thinking in hundreds, at the very most, thousands—you know, we might in six months sell maybe five thousand records instead of two thousand, or something like that. I started to record myself, since I basically liked my way of playing. Also, it was cheaper for me, as a producer, to hire me as pianist than someone else.

"We put the record [*Piano Rags by Scott Joplin*] out in November of 1970 and we instantly had a very enthusiastic response to it. We didn't spend a penny on promotional publicity—never have—but it just took off. I think it took about a year and then it was on the best-seller lists. It was really quite astonishing. I was pressed to make a second album, but didn't do so for a year and a half; I felt we shouldn't have too much ragtime in our catalogue. In the meantime Bill Bolcom had come into our fold and he did a record [*Heliotrope Bouquet*]. I didn't want to overdo it; I didn't want to push a fad or anything. At the time I said that I wouldn't do another album at all. And I didn't until it became ridiculous not to do one. So the second one [*Volume Two*] came out in 1972 and we were now number one on the classical charts. That's when I did my first concerts, too. . . . I went on tour in 1973 all around the country; in 1974 I toured England. After that I took myself out of circulation. The thing was becoming too big and was pressing me; I didn't have time to do other things; it was robbing me of all my time. So I made my plans to retire in 1974. After all, I was keeping on another career full time throughout all of this, that of a traditional academic musician. That's really what I come from and what I essentially am. There are those who have said to me, 'You'd give up all that exciting, lucrative stuff just to teach in the university and earn very little money and do research in musty libraries?' and so forth. I'd say, 'I'm afraid so.' It all depends on what you feel the happiest doing. I like the money, but I'm not going to change my life for it.

"I made my third record of Joplin [*Volume Three*] basically for myself. When I made the first one I hadn't really played the piano much in six or seven years, but on the last one I had been playing regularly in concert. Having an audience to work with is a very important education. You just play the instrument better. It's not a matter of the notes, it's a matter of extra precision, extra lightness, extra shading, this sort of thing. So I wanted finally to make one record that would represent my playing at its best once again, though, I held off doing it for a long time.

"It doesn't really make sense for me anymore. The three records I've made cover about two-thirds of the Joplin output. It's a solid thing there. That's enough."

Rifkin's recordings were a sensation of sorts; they not only made the classical charts but were also played on many of the underground listener-sponsored radio stations that at the time broadcasted in many larger cities. So Scott Joplin became a household name among the "hip" population. Rifkin soon began appearing on programs for the intellectual minority ("Camera Three," Public Broadcasting System programs, etc).

In the meantime Vera Lawrence proceeded with the project of publishing the complete works of Joplin, and with the help of Max Morath, Trebor Tichenor, Mike Montgomery, and other members of the ragtime community she was able to obtain copies of all the known Joplin rags. Dick Zimmerman proved particularly helpful in the search for this rare music by publishing a list of the music she needed in the *Rag Times*. After this, music started coming in of its own accord, and people in all parts of the country were contributing. Vera told me that it was all very exciting, that it was a very inspiring human experience.

The Collected Works of Scott Joplin, a two-volume publication, appeared in 1971 amid what was becoming a Joplin mania. *The New York Times*'s prestigious classical-music critic, Harold Schonberg, devoted a large Sunday article to the Joplin renaissance, and Max Morath observed that "once Harold Schonberg said Joplin was all right, all these classical-music people, who had known about Joplin but disregarded him, decided he was a genius. These are the same people he was up against all his life."

Joplin continued to dominate the classical-music charts in the following year with the release of a recording by Gunther Schuller and a group of his students called the New England Conservatory Ragtime Ensemble. Schuller explained his association with the music:

"I've always been interested in ragtime because I've always had one foot in jazz as a professional musician and a composer and listened since I was a teenager. I knew most of the piano-roll reissues that came out; and I was aware of Joplin and Lamb and those people, but since I'm not a pianist (I play the French horn) I could never do anything about ragtime as a performing musician until the *Red Back Book* became available. And it became available in the form of a Xerox copy from Bill Russell that I got through Vera Lawrence. Then, of course, I started performing these ragtime orchestrations at the first opportunity I had, and I did so really with no sense of starting a "ragtime revival" or making a "hit" or anything like that. I just performed the music here at the New England Conservatory as an educational effort, because I felt that our students and our faculty and our audiences should know about ragtime and particularly Joplin. It is a kind of sad commentary on the way we neglect our own American cultural heritage that if you had asked musicians five years ago "Who is Scott Joplin?" hardly anybody would have been able to answer the question. So, in any event, I put some of Joplin's ragtime pieces right in the middle of an otherwise "classical" concert of American music of the turn of the century. And everybody was delighted. All the people were ooh-ing and ah-ing and saying, 'My God, this music is fantastic. What wonderful melodies—what rhythm! Why haven't we heard this before?'

"We tape all our concerts at the Conservatory and I happened to send a copy to Martin Williams at the Smithsonian. We're old friends. We used to work together on the *Jazz Review*, and he was one of the first people to make me aware of the great ragtime masters and their works. Martin was enthusiastic and evidently he started talking about it to other people, and in that way Vera Lawrence heard about our ragtime performances. Then some record companies got wind of the tapes—I really don't know exactly how or from whom. All I know is that several of the major record companies—Angel, Columbia, RCA—heard copies of the tape we had made at our school. . . . One day I got a call from Angel Records asking, 'How would you like to record for our label?'—and the rest is history, I guess.

"There were no scores for the *Red Back Book*; the Xeroxes I received consisted just of individual parts. It was hard to assess the orchestrations until we had played them through. At the first rehearsal I saw that these were "stock arrangements" in which the melody is doubled many times; indeed everything is doubled— everything is done to "play safe." These orchestrations were made for every conceivable combination, so that if you didn't have a flute, the melody would be played by the violin; if you didn't have

Conductor Gunther Schuller and his New England Conservatory musicians in rehearsal preparation for their recording of Scott Joplin rags. Photograph courtesy of Angel Records.

a violin, it would be played on the cornet; if you didn't have any of these, then the melody would be played by the right hand of the piano; and so on. So all I did was a certain "weeding out" of the instrumentations or editing. I did that for our first concert and that, I suppose, contributed to the interest on the part of the record company executives. In this form the arrangements featured solos (although rarely), more often duets and trios and quartets, and, of course, also full ensembles. I also put in dynamics, because there were very few in the original *Red Back Book*.

"Our Angel record sold over sixty thousand in the first two or three months. Then one day I was called by George Roy Hill, the film producer. He was very excited about our ragtime record. He said he'd heard it a few times, had loved it, and since he was just starting on a new picture, *The Sting*, wanted in the worst way to have this kind of ragtime music as a background score, and would I do the score for the film. As it turned out I couldn't do it because I was engaged at the time, as I am every summer, at Tanglewood as director of the Boston Symphony's summer school. He wanted me to drop everything and come out to Hollywood for three weeks. I told him I couldn't do that—and that's how Marvin Hamlisch got the job. They were obliged to use my editions and arrangements—the original arrangements with my editings—because in the meantime we had copyrighted them to protect them from unlicensed use. And that's why on *The Sting* sound track record it says 'arranged by Gunther Schuller.' Marvin Hamlisch then, of course, got the Oscar for music he didn't write (since it is by Joplin) and arrangements he didn't write, and "editions" he didn't make. A lot of people were upset by that, but that's show biz!"

Joshua Rifkin was also approached to do the score for *The Sting* and turned it down because of time commitments. He says:

> The score for *The Sting* is a direct stylistic lift from two sources: *The Red Back Book* on the one hand and my records on the other. . . . Gunther's style of performance is *completely* different from mine. . . . What you get in the movie is piano solos played exactly like mine and the orchestral arrangements done exactly like his. The sound-track version of "The Entertainer"—that sudden speeding up of the tempo and so on—is . . . what a tape editor could do by crosscutting sections from our two records.*

Commercially at least, Marvin Hamlisch was the most important figure in the revival of Joplin's music. As I write this it seems almost silly to recount how omnipresent the theme from *The Sting*,

---

* John Kronenberger, "Ragtime Revival—A Belated Ode to Composer Scott Joplin," *New York Times*, August 11, 1974, p. D4. © 1974 by The New York Times Company. Reprinted by permission.

Joplin's "The Entertainer," was in 1974 and 1975, but for the sake of future historians who might be reading this volume, I will try to present a picture.

THE JOPLIN INDUSTRY

"The Entertainer" became number one on nearly all the charts. Whereas none of those spineless trend watchers who program our radio listening for us would give Joplin's music a scintilla of air time before, they all pounced on it as soon as Hollywood gave it its blessing. And so we were inundated with Joplin—or was it Joplin? Somehow amid the furor the composer's name and that of the composition got lost. "And now [for the fortieth time today] here is the theme from *The Sting*, by Marvin Hamlisch," announced our local DJ. Fact: One local television game show in Columbus, Ohio, ironically called *In the Know*, which quizzes high school students on a variety of topics, played "The Entertainer" and asked for the name of the composer. One student responded "Scott Joplin"—and was counted *wrong*! Their correct answer was *Marvin Hamlisch*!

From what I could see, Hamlisch was really doing alright for himself that year.* He had won four Grammies and three Oscars —two for his music for *The Way We Were* and one for his adaptation of Joplin's music for *The Sting*. At twenty-nine these awards climaxed an already astonishing career of musical acclaim: At the age of eight he was the youngest person ever to attend Juilliard; at seventeen he had a hit song on the rock charts in Leslie Gore's "Sunshine, Lollipops, and Rainbows" (for her father's Mercury label); at nineteen he was working in New York with his high school chum Liza Minnelli; then he became assistant vocal arranger for *Funny Girl*. He spent three years as musical director for *The Bell Telephone Hour*, and shortly thereafter at the age of twenty-four moved to Hollywood, where he continued a career already begun at twenty as a film composer. Movie

---

* This is all, I'm sorry to say, second-hand information, for Mr. Hamlisch was the only person that I attempted to contact for this book who was completely inaccessible. Success, it would seem, gives rise to a protective breed of managers, bookers, and secretaries.

credits included *Bananas, Take the Money and Run,* and *Kotch,* for which he received an Academy Award nomination. Hamlisch also spent some time on tour as accompanist to Groucho Marx and was reportedly held in high esteem by the theatrical crowd because he was able to keep Groucho, who had recently suffered a stroke, on the right track during an important Carnegie Hall performance. All in all a pretty good track record.

In one sense it's possible to see Hamlisch as the perfect choice to represent Joplin in the 1970s: If we assume (as do many scholars) that Joplin was trying to escape from his past and attain some incorruptible ideal of puritanical perfection—then Marvin Hamlisch is in many ways the logical selection for the job. He had legitimacy from the musical establishment right from the beginning; he had a string of successes, no major failures, and as near as I can figure has never been touched with the taintings of sin that haunted Joplin. As Hamlisch says, "A congressional investigating committee would have a hard time coming up with any dirt." Marvin doesn't smoke (anything), doesn't drink, and according to one article, has only been "in love" once in his life for a short time when he was twenty-two.*

There was an unresolved question in the minds of many ragtime enthusiasts as to whether *The Sting* helped or hurt the cause. In spite of Hamlisch's insistence that he had helped Joplin by publicizing his music, it seemed doubtful that the old master had benefited much. And as Turk Murphy would often say in introducing "The Entertainer," "Maybe *The Sting* helped Scott Joplin, but we shouldn't forget that Scott Joplin's music also helped *The Sting* quite a bit." (Turk gave me a bumper sticker that states succinctly: "Scott Joplin Got Stung.")

There is no question but that Joplin became familiar to vast numbers of people during the boom, and there was a great deal of enthusiasm generated for recording ragtime for a while. But in the minds of the public Joplin's music became crystallized with the same rigid expectations that had previously stereotyped it in the honky-tonk days of the nineteen fifties. Only now the shrill voices that used to demand the "Maple Leaf Rag" insisted on "The Sting." "The Entertainer" thus joined the ranks of "The Saints"

* Ira Mayer, "Challenging Success Head On," *Record World,* July 26, 1975.

and "Bill Bailey" (and maybe "Proud Mary" for you rock 'n' rollers) as background for the consumption of alcohol. During the peak years of the fad the record companies had inundated the market with rip-off performances: Every available artist (and I use the term here loosely) who could muster up any sort of rendition of Joplin had been pressed into service with the resulting deluge of largely imitative and tasteless crap. Some performers who otherwise might have been able to do justice to Joplin's work if given enough time were rushed to turn out albums before the boom went bust. And many, many performers whose natural bent was completely alien to this music cranked out an album or two as well. My own choice for the absolute "pits" among the heap is an album called *Gatsby's World/Turned-On Joplin*, which contains electronic-synthesizer renditions of the classic rags. I am not against electronic music—but for me these particular interpretations are devastatingly effective in robbing the music of its inherent dignity and subtlety.

There was, on the other hand, some wheat among the chaff. One especially deserving recording to come from the legion of classical artists who undertook the challenge of this music was a collaboration by violin virtuoso Itzhak Perlman and pianist André Previn. Their album of Joplin rags, entitled *The Easy Winners*, appeared in 1975, too late to cash in on the fad; but they had obviously given their work some real attention and respect. They were in command of the music. There was no slavish adherence to the printed page, but the intent of the composer had been maintained with skill and imagination. It made me wonder what would have happened if someone like Horowitz or Rubinstein had turned his energies to ragtime.

The works of most of the other great classic-rag composers besides Joplin were recorded during this time, but none of their music really caught on. In many cases I think this was because so few performers who attempted the projects were equal to the task. It takes a while to learn ragtime, and very few seemed to have put in the hours necessary to learn the discipline in depth. Where I have seen the most conscientious effort is in the young people who are starting to really dig into the music and learn it from the ground up.

A group of original composers began to surface in the 1970s: In addition to the previously mentioned William Bolcom and William Albright could be added the names of Peter Lundberg and Donald Ashwander. The pity is that there are not many more who recorded. I discovered in traveling around the United States that there are hundreds of magnificent rags being composed all over the country, but few are likely ever to be heard.

Likewise, few of the talented young ragtime players I have heard in the last few summers are likely to get much exposure. Just for example I heard last year a trio consisting of guitar, mandolin, and violin called The Et Cetera String Band who are playing very exciting renditions of rags by composers from their home town, Kansas City. It's great stuff, but the last I heard they were on the point of disbanding for lack of support. Et Cetera is, of course, up against the same commercial market-glutting that characterized the Tin Pan Alley of the original ragtime era. But in those days it was ragtime music in general that was overworked. Now it had become the music of the one man, Joplin, that was driven into the ground.

In this decade "Joplinia" has been dispensed in every conceivable manner: The record stores, for a time, featured special up-front displays of Joplin records; scads of Joplin folios have appeared in the music stores; nearly all the radio stations were playing Joplin; Joplinesque music is still being composed for television commercials; there are Scott Joplin T-shirts, mugs, and bumper stickers; someone even marketed a Scott Joplin write-your-own-rag-by-the-throw-of-the-dice game; Joplin has been played on pianos, zithers, synthesizers, theater organs, guitars, harpsichords, by orchestras, string quartets, singers, and bands beyond reckoning. Now, the media people knew well before 1975 that Joplin's commercial potential was nearly exhausted. When Marvin Hamlisch copped the movie trophy in February of 1974—that was the zenith, and the beginning of the end. Shortly thereafter the long-range trend predictors saw the early signs of a fading star and in another year or so the rest of us also realized that the trip was over. As of the beginning of 1976, a few Joplin records could once again be found at the back of the record store under subheading "Ragtime," heading, "Jazz."

TREEMONISHA: HERE AND GONE

If the supercommercialization of Joplin and subsequent abandonment by the public did not finish off the legendary genius for
this decade, then the merchandizing of his fragile attempt at
opera did.

The first complete performance of *Treemonisha,* for which T. J.
Anderson with the help of Bill Bolcom labored four years, was
presented in Atlanta, Georgia, on January 28 and 29, 1972 at the
Atlanta Symphony Hall. Assembled for the occasion were most of
the hard-core ragtime enthusiasts, including Eubie Blake, Max
Morath, Dick Zimmerman, and Larry Melton. There were also
present, of course, those people responsible for the production,
including Bill Bolcom, who first brought the work to the attention
of Anderson and Vera Lawrence; Robert Shaw, director, and
Katherine Dunham, the distinguished black choreographer. The
music critics, including Harold Schonberg from *The New York
Times,* were also well represented.

The evening was filled with the tension and excitement of opening night. The first act was slow, and there was fear that maybe it
wasn't going to work. But at some point things fell into place and
at the conclusion, as Schonberg noted in his review, "the audience
tonight went out of its mind after hearing 'A Real Slow Drag.' "*
The critics were unanimous in praising the production, most calling special attention to the dance sequences. *Time* magazine said:

> It [*Treemonisha*] turned out to be of far more than historical
> interest. Despite its naïveté the opera brims with jubilant
> rhythms and haunting melodies. . . . Katherine Dunham treated
> *Treemonisha* as the period piece it is but did little more than
> use it as a frame for big dance scenes. These had a scalp-tin-
> gling power. The gorgeous "A Real Slow Drag" ended the
> opera with a ceremonious eroticism that nearly matched Jop-
> lin's music.**

* Harold C. Shonber, "Music: *Treemonisha,*" *New York Times,* January 31, 1972.
** "From Rags to Rags," *Time,* February 7, 1972, p. 89. Reprinted by
permission from TIME, The Weekly Newsmagazine; Copyright Time Inc.

The audience and critics were satisfied with the performance, but the controllers of the copyright were not. And who were the controllers of the copyright? The Music Trust of Lottie Joplin Thomas (Joplin's second wife, who died in 1955) claimed it was them. And who were the members of the trust? No one quite knew for sure at the time, but the advisor for the trust was Vera Brodsky Lawrence, who was apparently dissatisfied with the T. J. Anderson orchestration, enough so to have Bill Bolcom do another one for the next performance. "Against my better judgment," says Bolcom, "I was told that if I didn't do it, the job would go to a Broadway hack. I'd had nothing against T.J.s orchestrations." When it was presented in August the same year at Wolf Trap Farm outside of Washington, D.C., critical response was mixed. One article, by Byron Belt of the Newhouse News Service, headlined "Ragtime Great's Opera Disappoints Reviewer" stated:

> The composer's dialogue and his characters tend toward caricature. Joplin's simple sincerity, however, could easily carry the burden of dated language and sermonizing if only the production had real faith in either the creator or his creation.*

Very little more was heard of the opera for the next few years. The controllers of the trust of Lottie Joplin effectively barred any further performances.** T. J. Anderson, who was interested in establishing from the *Treemonisha* royalties a Scott Joplin Foundation for the furtherance of Afro-American music through scholarships, was particularly upset. As he said, "Ninety-eight percent of pop music comes from the black community, but not two percent of the money is ever returned there." †
The resulting acrimony over the dropping of Anderson's score

---

* Byron Belt, "Ragtime Great's Opera Disappoints Reviewer," *New Orleans Times-Picayune*, August 20, 1972.
** Jack Viertel, "Scott Joplin: His Rags, Whose Riches?" *New Times*, November 29, 1974.
† Claude Lewis, "An Opinion from the *Philadelphia Bulletin*," December 8, 1974.

had ruined the friendship of Bolcom and Anderson, and Bolcom was now sorry he had done the thing. He later stated:

> Vera Lawrence is a tragic figure who might have done more harm than good for the composer. The sad part is that I don't think she meant to do irreparable harm to Joplin. But she did by tying up his opera with legal maneuvering."*

The trust also turned down an offer by Columbia Records to record the complete opera, and Twentieth Century-Fox was rejected in a bid to reproduce some selections in a television movie.** In spite of all requests, *Treemonisha* remained unperformed throughout the height of the Joplin craze brought on by *The Sting*. Finally a new production was planned for 1975. *The New York Times* carried an announcement:

> When Scott Joplin's opera, *Treemonisha*, was mounted in Atlanta a few years ago and proved to be a quite substantial and effective work, everyone tried to get into the act. This included many people who wanted to put it on as a Broadway show, with the idea of making a quick buck out of it.
>
> To Vera Brodsky Lawrence, who had edited the score for publication, this was nothing short of sacrilege. Although she admires and loves Joplin's ragtime pieces, which have become so popular in recent years (she has edited these, too), she insists that *Treemonisha* is a valid opera. Fortunately the copyright was owned by a trust in Joplin's widow's name. She died in the 1950s and her heir, a niece, has renewed the copyright.
>
> Well, *Treemonisha* is going to be staged again, this time with a brand new orchestration by Gunther Schuller. He is particularly qualified to supply this because he is a composer and because he is immersed in the Joplin idiom as conductor of the New England Conservatory Ragtime Ensemble.
>
> The new production will be done in Houston by its local opera company during its annual free season in the Miller Out-

---

* Leslie Carole Johnson, "A Popular History," *Mississippi Rag*, November 1975, p. 2.

** Viertel, "Scott Joplin."

door Theater. There will be seven performances, beginning May 23. The stage director will be Frank Corsaro. The designer, Franco Collevecchia, will model his sets after Romare Bearden's paintings, and Schuller will conduct. *

I found it interesting that after this attack on the quick-buck Broadway entrepreneurs, the Houston production was taken in its entirety to Broadway, and in a preperformance writeup of *Treemonisha*, *New York Magazine*'s Alan Rich informed his readers:

Remembering the fate of certain other Broadway shows for which that lethal word "opera" has been involved, the New York producers have begged me to leave it out of this article. **

Vera Lawrence is quoted in the same article:

I must admit . . . that I too had some doubts about *Treemonisha* at one time. The other performances were, shall we say, spotty. . . . Now Gunther has restored the work to exactly its proper perspective. . . . The thing about *Treemonisha* now is that it's so full of love. . . . All these new people, Gunther, Frank and the rest, have brought their own love to the piece. It's going to work, you'll see.

After the opening of the new production in Houston, *Treemonisha* was played in Washington, D.C., on its way to Broadway's Uris Theater. Reviewer Richard L. Coe compared it with the former Wolftrap production and concluded that the new version accented form over originality at the cost of vitality. † I agreed with him after I witnessed the opening night in Houston and compared it to what I had seen in Atlanta a few years before.

---

* "*Treemonisha*," *New York Times*, December 15, 1974. © 1974 by The New York Times Company. Reprinted by permission.

** "Premonitions of *Treemonisha*," September 8, 1975, p. 57. Copyright © 1975 by the NYM Corp. Reprinted with the permission of NEW YORK Magazine.

† Richard L. Coe, "Two Works at Once Old and 'New' at the Kennedy Center," *Washington Post*, September 14, 1975, p. H3.

The Atlanta production, while performed in part by students, nevertheless took Joplin at his word, emphasizing the unique Afro-American aspects of the work rather than the European grand-opera traditions. The Houston production had lost most of the simple folk qualities, especially of the dance, and was instead turned into a semiballet with highly stylized sets. Once again the balance of opposing forces in Joplin's music had been tilted in favor of the nineteenth-century classicism of Europe.

The advance publicity for the Houston production stressed "authenticity." David Gockley, the Houston Grand Opera's general director, explained that the two recent tries at *Treemonisha* had failed because of "unsuitable orchestration and inferior production values." To rectify the situation Gockley (actually Vera Lawrence, according to all other accounts) had enlisted the talents of "the greatest ragtime music scholar in the world," Gunther Schuller, and other "brilliant men to tackle the assignments of stage direction and set and costume design."*

For all this, I, for one at least, questioned whether this production was superior in authenticity or quality to the previous attempts, and I was curious as to why no one else had been doing any of this music. As it turned out, the ultimate success or failure of *Treemonisha* was not in the hands of the artists so much as lawyers. Upon the death of Lottie Joplin in 1955, the Joplin estate was turned over to the Lottie Joplin Thomas trust fund with a lawyer, Robert Rosborne, as trustee. There was in 1975 one surviving descendant of Lottie—a niece, Mrs. Mary Warmley. This fact Vera Lawrence must have discovered in doing research on the publication of the Joplin works. Lawrence and her lawyer, Alvin Deutsch, then began acting as advisors to the estate in association with Mr. Rosborne. The exact arrangement was unknown, but the net result was the trust's assertion of control over who would and who would not perform the opera. Hence, the three-year absence of any performance during the crest of the Joplin fad.

The whole business finally came to a head when the trust threatened to sue Olympic Records over the inclusion of several numbers from *Treemonisha* in a 1974 five-record set recorded

---

* Publicity release by Houston Grand Opera as reprinted by *Rag Times*, 9, no. 2 (July 1975): p. 1.

by Dick Zimmerman—the same Dick Zimmerman, incidentally, who had published the list of needed rags in *The Rag Times* for Lawrence's Joplin publication.

When first contacted and informed that they had no legal right to record the *Treemonisha* material, Olympic offered to repackage the album without it, but Deutsch insisted on a $3,500 fee ($2,500 in damages and $1,000 in legal fees, in exchange for not suing the company). Instead of paying this, the president of the company decided to investigate the legal rights of the estate to prohibit recordings. He discovered that the numbers had been previously recorded in 1971 for a special sale at the Lincoln Center Library and by various other artists. According to copyright law, only the first recorded performance needs a license from the copyright holder. Olympic sued for $750,000 (reputation, damages, etc.); and the trust countersued in federal court for copyright infringement.

Meanwhile Mary Warmley was interviewed by a representative of Olympic and was discovered to be an elderly woman, a former domestic, who was unaware that *The Sting* had ever existed, did not own a phonograph, and had never heard Joplin's music. When asked about the money she was making from the various royalties from the music, she said that every once in a while her lawyer, Mr. Rosburne, would take her to the bank and give her what she needed.

There were more lawsuits. The Lottie Joplin Thomas trust only spoke for the rights of Scott Joplin the *composer*; the rights of Scott Joplin the *publisher*, on the other hand, were theoretically controlled by someone else. And of course there was a conflict. According to copyright records in the United States, *Treemonisha* is controlled by the estate of Wilbur Sweatman, a musician friend of Joplin. When Sweatman died, his illegitimate daughter tried to pick up the copyright but couldn't, as New York State does not recognize illegitimate children. It then went to his sister, Eva Sweatman, who died some years later, leaving the estate to her friend, Robert Sweeney. As of 1975 the books of ASCAP showed the Wilbur Sweatman Music Publishing Company (Robert Sweeney) still receiving money on *Treemonisha* and not the Lottie Joplin estate. Sweeney offered half of his rights on *Treemonisha* to the head of Olympic Records if he would follow their lawsuit against the Lottie Joplin Trust to a successful conclusion. As of this writing, the case was scheduled for hearing by the New York State Supreme Court.*

It appears that we may never get a chance to evaluate the full potential of *Treemonisha* because of what actually amounts to the effective censorship of its free interpretation. Joplin never had the chance himself to experiment with the production, but maybe someone else might have been able to, possibly cutting it down to a shorter work. It would be a sad thing indeed if any one of the interpretations of Joplin's rags had been the only one permitted to be heard, but that, in effect, is what has happened to his most ambitious effort. It seems a safe bet that it will now be returned to the lifeless library shelves and museums from which it was retrieved for such a short time.

It is not my intention to give the impression that ragtime music is now extinct with the collapse of the Joplin/*Sting* vogue. There were too many seeds of interest planted and too many creative veins left untapped for it to be put completely to rest. For one thing, as I write this, The E. L. Doctorow best-selling novel *Ragtime* is about to be made into a high-budgeted motion picture to be directed by Robert Altman of *M.A.S.H.* and *Nashville* fame. This will likely give the music some kind of push.

For another thing, ragtime seems to keep turning up unexpectedly in the performances of unlikely artists such as Woody Guthrie's son, Arlo, who wrote an excellent rag called "Week on the Rag," and Maria Muldaur, who has explored the roots of ragtime with some of her recordings, such as "Work Song." "Hurricane Hamlisch" has passed, but the foundations of real ragtime still stand in its wake. The whole field of ragtime knowledge has been greatly expanded as a result of the new scholarly interest generated during this period. In 1974 and 1975 Scott Joplin festivals were held in Sedalia, Missouri, which, with the organization of Larry Melton, provided a most pleasant atmosphere in which musicians and scholars alike could exchange ideas. And there was some new publishing activity begun in the 1970s, notably an excellent monthly periodical, *The Mississippi Rag* (5644 Morgan Avenue, South, Minneapolis, Minnesota 55419), which continues to publish a diversity of well-written articles.

* This information was given to me by an executive of Olympic Records.

11

Some Concluding Thoughts

When I first started telling my friends that I was writing a book about ragtime, the most common response I got was something like, "Oh, you're going to write about the sex life of a ragtime piano player?" To which I would respond with something like, "No, it's not going to be that interesting." But lo and behold, as I began to explore some of the more current literature on ragtime, I discovered that sex *is* a relevant issue here.

Rudi Blesh, in an introduction for a 1973 volume of ragtime music, wrote:

> It [ragtime] bloomed in the lurid nights of those inner cities of the '90s, the infamous red light districts of brothels, saloons, casinos and wine rooms.
>
> Today, with pornography everywhere, the tenderloin milieu of ragtime development might be construed as one of the prime reasons for its current rediscovery and new acceptance. But this would be a sad error to make, even if ragtime had in truth been soiled by its youthful associations. To the contrary; Scott Joplin's justly famous "Maple Leaf Rag" is an affirmation not of blatant sexuality but of pure, triumphant musicality.*

Taking another stand on the issue, authors William Schafer and Johannes Riedel, in their 1973 book, *The Art of Ragtime*, viewed

---

* Rudi Blesh, ed., *Classic Piano Rags* (New York: Dover Publications, 1973), p. v.

some of the classic ragtime as profoundly sexual. They conclude that "only an innocent composer like Joseph Lamb would attempt to describe 'American Beauty' through highly suggestive sexual images in its bass part," and they cite as an example in this rag the "sixteenth-note progressions in contrary motion to the right hand" that supposedly represent coitus.*

I had a great deal of trouble in seeing a direct relationship between Lamb's rag and screwing, but I think there is a point to be made here about the sexuality—or sensuality—of ragtime in general. I have included quotes throughout this volume to illustrate that most of the older ragtime composers and players were, to a great extent, creatures of the flesh. And the reason I did this was not simply to spice up the text and sell more books (although I'm certainly not against that) but because I sense in recent years the tendency to try to deny this physical aspect of the music and imbue it with the most sterile qualities of classicism.

Our respected institutions of musical culture such as Juilliard now accept Scott Joplin as a legitimate composer, although they still generally reject jazz. And why? Because Joplin is now seen as *rejecting* his past associations with the sensual and accepting the higher standards of "pure" music—the refined concert hall; in other words, he cleaned up his act. According to Rifkin:

> The argument that it [ragtime] is good-time music that belongs in saloons and places like that is pure rubbish. Ragtime grew up in these places, but Joplin was not writing for these places. He was writing a consciously stylized music for concert performance. . . .
>
> It is not dance music at all. It is dance music in the sense that its roots are in dance music but it is *Not* music to be danced to. It's music to be listened to just as much as a Beethoven symphony is to be listened to. That you can dance to it is neither here nor there. . . .
>
> This is one place I would be very categoric. Joplin was working *from* a folk realm but it was not what he was working *to*. And ragtime does not belong in the folk realm. It is just not all of those things. That's not a value judgment—it's just a

---

* (Baton Rouge, La.: Louisanna State University Press, 1973), p. 66.

simple matter of definition. Folk music is a basically improvisatory tradition. It is not in any way as refined or sophisticated as Joplin. *

Ragtime historian Sam Charters would go even one step further in removing Joplin from his background. He told me that he was convinced from going through all the old newspaper articles on Joplin that he had never set foot in a whorehouse. (His syphilis was apparently congenital.) In any case, the current scholarly view is that Joplin worked all his life to erase the stigma of his early "low-down" associations. He's alright because he tried to get away from all that Sin and into the concert hall. A few facts have to make us stop and think about these assertions, however.

Joplin could have played concerts, as did "Blind" Boone, whom he knew, but he didn't. There are numerous documentations of occasions where he played for dances—but I can find no instance of his performing solo piano in concert.

And Joplin relates his music to the dance. "The Ragtime Dance" is more than just an imitation of dance music for the concert stage—it *is* dance music. It has directions for dancing. In our headlong rush to bring Joplin to the concert halls we have forgotten that ragtime was overtly functional as music for bodily movement. It was a highly physical celebration of the sensual present. Joplin's clear goal, it seems to me, was not to abandon and forget this aspect of it but to have it accepted. He was not working *from* folk music *to* concert music, nor from the saloon and bordello to the concert stage. He was working toward the goal of tearing down the barriers, a goal that is still elusive. Ragtime came from the lusty, unsophisticated folkways and finally made it to the ranks of legitimacy. But the new practitioners would cleanse it of all traces of its virile past.

As we've seen, certain musicians and critics are neatly polarized on the question of where ragtime properly belongs; Bob Darch, for instance, stoutly defends the saloons, and Joshua Rifkin stands by the halls of academe. But the question of ragtime's proper

* Leslie Carole Johnson, "Rifkin on Ragtime," *Mississippi Rag*, March 1975, pp. 2–3.

The author with Eubie Blake, 1970

home is only one of many that have been argued since Joplin's day.

The following is a sampling of opinion and comment. We begin in 1915 with Axel Christensen, head of the Christensen School, ragtime entertainer, and publisher of *The Ragtime Review*, to which John Stark made frequent contributions. In this publication Christensen wrote what I could consider fairly good advice to serious students of ragtime piano:

> If you want to play real ragtime and play it well, do the following: Train and develop your touch until you can produce a firm, full, rounded tone.

Learn to shade your tones from loud to soft as the requirements of the piece and your interpretation of it may require.

Be sure to acquire a precise, even tempo, because a fluctuating tempo will kill the snappy, pulsating rhythm which is so desirable and so delightful in real ragtime.*

This last point has drawn some serious opposition in recent years. The 1970s have seen some very respected ragtime authorities, including Max Morath, sanction the use of tempo changes, whether annotated or not, within the music. Rudi Blesh says:

> The functional use of ragtime to accompany marching and dancing . . . insured a fixed tempo, just as minuet and gavotte were so governed in their day. Nevertheless, not only is *rubato* implicit in classic ragtime . . . but *ritardandi* and *accelerandi* in melodic turns and in cadences seem so obviously pertinent that they are an accepted part of serious ragtime playing today. . . .** A page from Lamb or the mature Joplin (like a page from Chopin) seems to cry out for the quickening of a pulse here and the tender prolonging of a phrase there. . . .†

Blesh gave the impression during a recorded interview that Joe Lamb was leaning toward an abandonment of regular tempo and strict adherence to the printed score in his later years.‡ This was not confirmed by Lamb's wife, Amelia, who said, "Joe never changed tempo within the rags. They should be played slowly and regular 'like the ticking of a clock.'" She also added that Lamb insisted on the scores being played exactly as written.

We have the recordings of Lamb playing his own works, which document his wife's contentions. We also have some documentation of Joplin's playing. Fortunately, the latter recorded at least

---

* Axel Christensen, "Tone and Touch for Ragtime," *Ragtime Review* (Chicago), July 1915, p. 5.
** Vera Brodsky Lawrence, ed., *Scott Joplin Collected Piano Works* (New York: New York Public Library, 1971), p. xx.
† Rudi Blesh, *Classic Piano Rags* (New York: Dover Publications, 1973), p. viii.
‡ Milton Kaye, *The Classic Rags of Joe Lamb* (New York: Golden Crest Records, 1975), CRS-4127.

six hand-played piano rolls that provide us with actual samples of his playing in all aspects except dynamics. These along with the recollections of Charlie Thompson, Arthur Marshall, and Eubie Blake indicate several things about his style:

1. Joplin rarely deviated from the printed score in melody but did add nonmelodic ornaments to the performance. He seems to have been especially fond of adding left-hand sixteenth-note runs or grace notes. These generally filled in, rather than changed, the printed score. For example,

"Weeping Willow"—Joplin's original score

"Weeping Willow"—Joplin piano-roll interpretation

2. The meter was rigidly maintained with rhythmic tension created by a slight anticipation in the left hand and the sometimes breaking up of chords into linear patterns; Joplin's recording of W. C. Handy's "Ole Miss" provides an example of this. In the second measure of the *A* strain he plays the whole-note chord in the right hand as an irregular ragtime pattern rather than the whole-note chord as written. Example:

Original score

Joplin interpretation

3. Joplin generally performed his pieces slowly, but in a conversation with Trebor Tichenor in 1959, Arthur Marshall commented that Joplin would sometimes play much faster for exhibitions.

4. I have been able to find no evidence whatsoever that Joplin added *rubato*, or change of tempo, between sections of his rags* as has become customary in their performance in recent days. One section of "Magnetic Rag," in fact, is marked *Tempo l'istesso* (the same tempo) as a warning to those who might be tempted to slow it up. One performer who sees fit to ignore Joplin's direction is Ann Charters. Her husband, Sam, says that the rag "cries out" for a change of tempo at that point; yet, as a "real purist," he does not approve of the interpretive changes that many other pianists have made in Joplin's works, including Bill Bolcom, Wally Rose, Paul Lingle, "Knocky" Parker, and Max Morath. He maintains the widely held opinion that the music should be played *exactly* as written.

On the other side of the fence is Dick Wellstood:

> I guess you could play the Joplin rags as written if you wanted to. I can't imagine why you should want to. If you think they're museum pieces, you could play them as written. Or if you're unable to improvise convincingly, you could play them as written. But they come out of—an Afro-American tradition; if there is such a thing then it has to do with improvisation and inflection. . . . Academic adherence to the written note—I can't see this. . . .
>
> I think the current Joplin revival is the victim of too many

---

* The one exception is the introduction to "Magnetic Rag," which starts at a slower tempo than that of the body of the piece.

academics; ragtime survived the assaults of the barroom pianists like me, but it's being inflected to death currently by the
Juilliard graduates.

Joplin is the genius, and his genius will survive all kinds of
assaults. Including this one by these Juilliard nit-wits. Those
rags have beautiful melodies, and you can really abuse them
and they'll still come out sounding well. I think that's happened in a number of cases—earlier the cats with the tacks and
hammers and now the cats with whatever *they* got. . . .

Rifkin:

I can't find a shred of evidence that leads me to suggest that
Joplin's music is not basically played as written. Obviously
one has to interpret the notated music with a certain amount
of understanding and sympathy, but all these statements or
romanticism that came from the jazz- and folk-tinged ideas has
absolutely nothing to do with musical reality. It's just not true
for Joplin. It's a music that was meant to be written. It is not
African music. There may have been African influences, but
it is primarily Western music, and Western music has a tradition of fundamentally being played as written. As far as I can
see, it's not meant to be played with any more liberty vis-a-vis
the written score than Mozart or Chopin.

Isaac Goldberg, in his book *Tin Pan Alley*, wrote in 1930:

Academic syncopation may be set down on paper. The notes
of ragtime, as of jazz, may be set down likewise, but unless
there is added that something which defies notation, one hears
sounds, not ragtime. Ragtime is in an aural, not a notational,
tradition. It has come down from ear to ear, not from sheet to
sheet. There is in it a gypsy quality that the Hungarian or the
Spaniard should understand.*

* Isaac Goldberg, *Tin Pan Alley* (New York: John Day Company, 1930),
pp. 143–144.

Rifkin, speaking on another point:

> The trick in Joplin is to maintain a rhythmic buoyancy and life and at the same time the speeds are slow and the expression is basically lyrical and inward.*

Johnny Maddox:

> Some of the new ragtime players make something depressing out of what should be kind of happy. They play the rags like dirges—they have no feeling whatsoever. I think they ought to be bright. I don't mean fast. I mean just have some *life* to them.

Turk Murphy:

> I feel very strongly that Scott Joplin and James Scott were actually early jazz musicians and . . . there's no getting away from the fact that jazz music has to be played with great feeling. And I don't think that anybody without a feeling for this sort of music should try to play ragtime. Rifkin is a fine pianist, but he's not exactly to my liking. . . .

Rifkin:

> I certainly can see that a lot of people would be (or would once have been) shocked by my style of playing. It's the old ragtime devotees who have not liked it—and I can understand that reaction very well. I can't agree with it though and would have to say very strongly that I think there's a mistake there.

My own opinion, for what it's worth, is this: Probably the single most salient feature of ragtime for me is its iconoclasm. I like the

---

* Leslie Carole Johnson, "Rifkin on Ragtime," *Mississippi Rag*, March 1975, p. 3.

fact that it doesn't fit easily into a category of music, and further, that its composers are a group of dissimilar individuals. What Joplin tried to do with it was really different from what Lamb tried to do and certainly far removed from Blake. I respect the fact that all performers will bring to the music their own roots, and very few of them classify themselves as pure ragtime players. Joshua Rifkin is an academic musician; Max Morath is an entertainer; and Turk Murphy is a jazzman.

So on a personal level we all bring the bias of our particular disciplines to the music; we begin to categorize and nail it down in terms of what we already know. But ragtime has resisted classification and continued to change throughout the many years, making strengths of its ambiguities. It doesn't belong to any group —it's music of the individual and of all groups. For me, that's the charm, the challenge, and the joy.

A Selected Discography

ANDERSON, T. J.
Classic Rags and Ragtime Songs. Smithsonian Collection P–12974.

ARPIN, JOHN
Concert in Ragtime. Scroll LSCR–101.
The Other Side of Ragtime. Scroll LSCR–103.
Ragtime Piano. (Canada) Harmony HES–6026.
Solo Jazz Piano. Eubie Blake Music EBM–10.

ASH, MARVIN
Honky Tonk Piano. Capitol T–188.
Marvin Ash. Jazz Man 335 (10").
The Jazz Piano of. Fairmont LPM 104.
Piano Ragtime of the Fifties. Herwin 404.

ASHWANDER, DONALD
Ragtime, A New View. Jazzology JCE–71.
Turnips. Upstairs UPST–1.

ATWELL, WINEFRED
Double 7. London 1573.

AUGUST, JAN
Piano Roll Blues. Mercury MG20147.

BALES, BURT
They Tore My Playhouse Down. Good Time Jazz L–12025.

BALL, KENNY
More Kenny Ball. Kapp KL1314.

THE BANJO SPECIALISTS
The Banjo Specialists. House of Ragtime HR1001.

BARBER, CHRIS
Elite Syncopations. (England) Columbia 33SX–1245.

BIGGS, E. POWER
Plays Scott Joplin. Columbia M–32495.
Volume Two. Columbia M–33205.

BILK, ACKER
A Stranger No More. Reprise 6031.

BLAKE, EUBIE
The Wizard of the Ragtime Piano. 20th Fox 3003.
The Marches I Played on the Old Ragtime Piano. 20th Fox 3039.
Golden Reunion in Ragtime. Stereoddities C–1900.
The Eighty-six Years of. Columbia C2S–847.
They All Played the Maple Leaf Rag. Herwin 401.
Piano Rolls Volume One. Biograph BLP–1011Q.
Piano Rolls Volume Two. Biograph BLP–1012Q.
Eubie Blake. Eubie Blake Music EBM–1.
Rags to Classics. Eubie Blake Music EBM–2.
Eubie Blake and His Friends. Eubie Blake Music EBM–3.
Sissle and Blake Volume One. Eubie Blake Music EBM–4.
Live Concert. Eubie Blake Music EBM–5.
Eubie Blake Introducing Jim Hession. Eubie Blake Music EBM–6.
Sissle and Blake Volume Two. Eubie Blake Music EBM–7.
Eubie Blake and His Proteges: Jim Hession, Mike Lipskin and Terry Waldo—Theatre de Lys Concert. Eubie Blake Music EBM–8.
Eubie Blake Song Hits with Eubie and His Girls: Emme Kemp, Mable Lee and Mary Louise. Eubie Blake Music EBM–9.

BOLCOM, WILLIAM
Heliotrope Bouquet. Nonesuch H–71257.
Pastimes and Piano Rags. Nonesuch H–71299.
Bolcom Plays His Own Rags. Jazzology JCE–72.
After the Ball. Nonesuch H–71304.

BOLLING, CLAUDE
Original Ragtime. (France) Philips 70.341.

BOSTON POPS
Fiedler in Rags. Polydor PD 6033.

BOWMAN, EUDAY L.
Piano Ragtime of the Forties. Herwin 403.

BREUER, HARRY
  The Happy Sound of Ragtime. Audio Fidelity AFSD 5912.
  What This Country Needs. Audio Fidelity AFSD 6265.

BUSCH, LOU
  Honky Tonk Piano. Capitol T–188.
  (see JOE FINGERS CARR, pseudonym).

BUSHKIN, JOE
  Joe Bushkin/Teddy Wilson. Rondo-Lette 845.

CAMPBELL, BRUN
  The Professors. Euphonic ESR 1201.
  Volume Two. Euphonic ESR 1202.

CANADIAN BRASS
  Rag-Ma-Tazz Canadian Brass. Boat Master Concert Series BMC 3004.

CARR, JOE FINGERS
  Bar Room Piano. Capitol T–280.
  Rough House Piano. Capitol T–345.
  And His Ragtime Band. Capitol T–443.
  Plays the Classics. Capitol T–649.
  Mister Ragtime. Capitol T–760.
  Honky Tonk Street Parade. Capitol T–809.
  The Hits of Joe Fingers Carr. Capitol T–2019.
  The World's Greatest Ragtime Piano Player. Warner Bros. 1386.
  Brassy Piano. Warner Bros. 1456.

CASTLE, JO ANN
  Ragtime Piano Gal. Dot DLP 3249.

CHARTERS, ANN
  A Joplin Bouquet. GNP Crescendo 9021.
  Five Classic Rags. Portents 3.
  Essay in Ragtime. Folkways FG 3453.
  The Genius of Scott Joplin. GNP Crescendo 9032.
  Scott Joplin and His Friends. Sonet SNTF 682.

CHRISTENSEN, STEEN
  A Danish Tribute to Classical Ragtime. LB Specialty LBS–1.

COLLECTIONS OF ORIGINAL RAGTIME PERFORMANCES ON 78 RPM
  Black and White Piano Ragtime. Biograph BLP–12047.
  I'll Dance Till the Sun Breaks Through. (England) Saydisc SDL–210.
  Piano Ragtime of the Teens, Twenties and Thirties. Herwin 402.

Piano Ragtime of the Forties. Herwin 403.
A Jazz Piano Anthology. Columbia KG 32355.
Piano Ragtime of the Fifties. Herwin 404.
A Programme of Ragtime. (England) Vintage Jazz Music VLP–1.
Ragged Piano Classics. Origin Jazz Library OJL–16.
Ragtime, A Recorded Documentary. Piedmont PLP–13158.
Ragtime, The City. RBF–17.
Ragtime, The Country. RBF–18.
Ragtime Entertainment. Folkways RBF–22.
Ragtime Piano Originals. Folkways RF–23.
Ragtime Piano Interpretations. Folkways RF–24.
String Ragtime. Yazoo L–1045.
They All Played the Maple Leaf Rag. Herwin 401.
Toe Tappin' Ragtime. Folkways RBF–25.
When Grandma Was a Teenager. (England) Vintage Jazz Music
VLP–2.

COHAN, GEORGE M.
George M. Cohan: Yankee Doodle Dandy. Olympic 7111.

COLYER, KEN
Ragtime Revisited. Joy 194.
Contemporary Ragtime Guitar. Kicking Mule 107.

CROZIER, HUGH
Piano Ragtime 1970. (England) Stomp ROBB 002.

DAPOGNY, JAMES
The Piano Music of Ferdinand "Jelly Roll" Morton. Smithsonian Collection N–003.

DARCH, BOB
Gold Rush Daze. Stereoddities C–1901.
Ragtime Piano. United Artists UAL–3120.

DAVIS, EDDY
Plays Ragtime. Pa Da 7401.
Just for Fun. Pa Da 7402.

DAVIS, PETE
Ragtime Piano. (England) Saydisc SDL–118.

DAWN OF THE CENTURY RAGTIME ORCHESTRA
Arcane AR–601.
Silks and Rags. Arcane AR–602.

DELANO, LOIS
 The Music of Joe Jordan. (Canada) Arpeggio 1205.

DICKIE, NEVILLE
 Ragtime Piano. (England) Saydisc SDL–118.
 Creative Ragtime. Euphonic ESR–1206.
 Introducing Neville Dickie. (England) Major Minor MCP–5039.
 I Love a Piano. (England) Major Minor SMCP–5054.
 A Salute to Fats Waller. (England) Columbia SCX–6445.
 Rags and Tatters. (England) Contour 2870–190.

THE DIXIELAND JUG BLOWERS
 Jugs, Washboards and Kazoos. RCA LPV–520.

DUGAN, AL "SPIDER"
 Please Don't Put Your Empties on the Piano. Warner Bros. 1329.

DUKES OF DIXIELAND
 Volume Eleven. Audio Fidelity AFSD–5928.

DUNCAN, HANK
 Hot Piano. (Switzerland) Ri Disc RD–4.
 Hank Duncan. 88 Up Right 001.
 A Tribute to James P. Johnson and Fats Waller. Hot Piano BS–6913.
 They All Played the Maple Leaf Rag. Herwin 401.

DYKSTRA, BRIAN
 American Beauty. Century Advent USR–5075.

EDEN ELECTRONIC ENSEMBLE
 Plugged in Joplin. (England) Pye 12101.

ERWIN, LEE
 Rosebud. Angel S–36075.

ET CETERA STRING BAND
 The Harvest Hop. Moon Records.

EUROPE, JAMES REESE
 Too Much Mustard. (England) Saydisc SDL–221.
 An Evening with Scott Joplin. New York Public Library NYPL-SJ.

EWELL, DON
 Pianist. Windin' Ball 101 (10″).
 Piano Solos of King Oliver Tunes. 88 Up Right 002.
 Piano Ragtime of the Forties. Herwin 403.

A Jazz Portrait of the Artist. Chiaroscuro CR–106.
Live at the 100 Club. (England) 77 Records. 77SEU 12/42.
Grand Piano. Exclusive 501.

FILMER, VIC
  The Saga of Vic Filmer. Jazzology JCE–58.

FOLDS, CHUCK
  It's Ragtime. Jazzways JW 106/4.

GLOVER, JOE
  That Ragtime Sound. Epic LN–3581.

GORDY, JOHN
  Poppa John Gordy's Ragtime Piano. RCA Victor LPM–1060.

GREEN, GEORGE HAMILTON
  The Xylophone Genius. Conservatory 7101–M.

GREENE, BOB
  A Tribute to Jelly Roll Morton. (Denmark) Storyville SLP–221.
  Jelly Roll Revisited. Fat Cat's Jazz 139.
  The World of Jelly Roll Morton. RCA ARL1–0504.

GUTHRIE, ARLO
  Last of the Brooklyn Cowboys. Reprise MS2142.

HAMLISCH, MARVIN
  The Sting: Original Motion Picture Soundtrack. MCA 390.
  The Entertainer. MCA 2115.

HANDY, PETE
  Honky Tonk Piano. Mercury MG–20344.

HERSH, PAUL AND DAVID MONTGOMERY
  The Great Ragtime Classics. RCA ARL1–0364.

HESSION, JIM
  Eubie Blake Introducing Jim Hession. Eubie Blake Music EBM–6.

HUG, ARMAND
  Rags and Blues. Golden Crest CR–3064.

HUNT, PEE WEE
  The Best of. Capitol DT 1853.

HYMAN, DICK
Plays Ragtime, Stomps and Stride. Protect 3 PR–5080.
Ferdinand "Jelly Roll" Morton. Columbia M–32587.
Charleston, James P. Johnson. Columbia M–33706.
Scott Joplin, The Complete Works for Piano. 5 discs. RCA CRL5–1106.

JACKSON, CLIFF
Hot Piano. (Switzerland) Ri Disc RD–5.
Carolina Shout. Black Lion BLP–30136.

JASEN, DAVID
Creative Ragtime. Euphonic ESR–1206.
Fingerbustin' Ragtime. Blue Goose 3001.
Rompin' Stompin' Ragtime. Blue Goose 3002.

JENSEN, JOHN
Piano Rags by James Scott. Genesis GS–1044.
Piano Rags by Joseph Lamb. Genesis GS–1045.
Zez Confrey Novelty Piano Solos. Genesis GS–1051.

JOHNSON, BUNK
Bunk and Lu. Good Time Jazz L–12023.
The Last Testament of a Great New Orleans Jazz Man. Columbia
GL520.

JOHNSON, DINK
The Professors. Euphonic ESR–1201.
Volume Two. Euphonic ESR–1202.

JOHNSON, JAMES P.
Father of the Stride Piano. Columbia CL–1780.
The Original James P. Johnson. Folkways FJ–2850.
The Jazz Makers. (Australia) Swaggie S–1211.
New York Jazz. Stinson SLP–21.
Piano Ragtime of the Teens, Twenties and Thirties. Herwin 402.
Piano Ragtime of the Forties. Herwin 403.
Parlor Piano Solos. Biograph BLP–1003Q.
Volume Two. Biograph BLP–1009Q.
Backwater Blues. Riverside 151.

JONES, HANK
This is Ragtime Now! ABC-Paramount 496.

JORDAN, JOE
Golden Reunion in Ragtime. Stereoddities C–1900.

KAYE, MILTON
    The Classic Rags of Joe Lamb. Golden Crest CRS–4127.
    Volume Two. Golden Crest CRS–31035.
    Ragtime at the Rosebud. Golden Crest CRS–31032.
    You Tell 'Em Ivories. Golden Crest CRS–31040.

KOVACS, STEPHEN
    Tiger on the Keys. Electra EKL–111.

KRENZ, BILL
    Oh Willie, Play That Thing. MGM E–184 (10").

LAIBMAN, DAVID, AND ERIC SCHOENBERG
    The New Ragtime Guitar. Asch AHS–3528.

LAMB, JOSEPH
    A Study in Classic Ragtime. Folkways FG–3562.

LAMBERT, DONALD
    Harlem Stride Pianists. (French) RCA 741 118/119.

LARSON, LEROY
    Banjo Ragtime. Banjar 1781.

LINGLE, PAUL
    They Tore My Playhouse Down. Good Time Jazz L–12025.
    Vintage Piano. Euphonic ESR–1203.
    Piano Ragtime of the Fifties. Herwin 404.

LIPSKIN, MIKE
    California Here I Come. Flying Dutchman FD–10140.

LIST, EUGENE
    The Banjo. (Music of Louis Moreau Gottschalk) Vanguard VRS–485.

LONDON FESTIVAL BALLET ORCHESTRA
    The Entertainer Ballet. Columbia M–33185.

MADDOX, JOHNNY
    Authentic Ragtime. Dot 102 (10").
    Ragtime By Request. Dot DLP 25633.

MAYERL, BILLY
    The King of Syncopation. (England) World Records SH 189.

MAYL, GENE
    Gene Mayl's Dixieland Rhythm Kings on Parade. Red Onion #1.

MITCHELL, BILL
> *Vintage Piano.* Euphonic ESR–1203.
> *Ragtime Recycled.* Ethelyn ER–1750.

MONTGOMERY, DAVID, AND CECIL LYTLE
> *Rags, Blues, the Boogie Bougaloo.* Klavier KS–533.

MORATH, MAX
> *A Scintillating Program.* Epic LN–24066.
> *Oh, Play That Thing.* Epic BN–26106.
> *At the Turn of the Century.* RCA LSO–1159.
> *The Best of Scott Joplin.* Vanguard VSD–39/40.
> *The World of Scott Joplin.* Vanguard SRV–310.
> *Volume Two.* Vanguard SRV–351.
> *Irving Berlin/The Ragtime Years.* Vanguard VSD–79346.

MORGAN, RUSS, AND EDDIE WILSER
> *Kitten on the Keys.* Decca DL–8746.

MORTON, JELLY ROLL
> *Library of Congress Recordings.* 8 discs. (Sweden) Classic Jazz Masters CJM 2–9; (Australia) Swaggie S–1213; (Italy) Rhapsody RHA6021; (Holland) Gaps 010.
> *And His Red Hot Peppers.* (France) RCA 730.599.
> *Volume Two.* (France) RCA 730.605.
> *Volume Three.* (France) RCA 731.059.
> *Volume Four.* (France) RCA 741.040.
> *Volume Five.* (France) RCA 741.054.
> *Volume Six.* (France) RCA 741.070.
> *Volume Seven.* (France) RCA 741.081.
> *Volume Eight.* (France) RCA 741.087.
> *New Orleans Memories.* Atlantic SD2–308.
> *Ferd "Jelly Roll" Morton.* (England) Fountain FJ–104.
> *1923/24.* Milestone M–47018.
> *Piano Rolls.* Biograph BLP–1004Q.
> *Piano Ragtime of the Teens, Twenties and Thirties.* Herwin 402.

MULDAUR, MARIA
> *Maria Muldaur.* Reprise MS 2148.

MURPHY, TURK
> *The Many Faces of Ragtime.* Atlantic SD–1613.
> *The Music of Jelly Roll Morton.* Columbia 559.

MORRIS, RANDY
> (see THE BANJO SPECIALISTS)

THE NEW ENGLAND CONSERVATORY RAGTIME ENSEMBLE
The Red Back Book. Angel S–36060.
More Scott Joplin Rags. Golden Crest CRS–31031.
The Road from Rags to Jazz. Golden Crest CRS–31042.

THE NEW LEVIATHAN ORIENTAL FOX-TROT ORCHESTRA
On the S.S. Leviathan. Camel Race Records 19325.

NEW ORLEANS RAGTIME ORCHESTRA
New Orleans Ragtime Orchestra. Pearl PLP–7.
Volume Two. Pearl PLP–8.
Arhoolie 1058.
Vanguard VSD–69/70.

NEW SUNSHINE JAZZ BAND
Old Rags. Flying Dutchman BDL1–0549.

NICHOLS, KEITH
Plays Scott Joplin. (England) One Up OU–2035.
Cat at the Keyboard. (England) One Up OU–2085.

NICHOLS, RED
Blues and Old-Time Rags. Capitol ST–2065.

OSSMAN, VESS L.
Kings of the Ragtime Banjo. Yazoo L–1044.

O'TOOLE, KNUCKLES
Plays the Greatest All-Time Ragtime Hits. Grand Award GA 33–373.
(see DICK HYMAN, pseudonym)

PARENTI, TONY
Ragtime. Jazzology J–15.
Ragtime Jubilee. Jazzology J–21.

PARKER, KNOCKY
Piano Artistry. Audiophile AP–28.
Old Rags. Audiophile AP–49.
The Complete Piano Works of Scott Joplin. Audiophile AP–71/72.
The Complete Piano Works of James Scott. Audiophile AP–76/77.
The Complete Piano Works of Jelly Roll Morton. Audiophile AP–102/105.
Golden Treasury of Ragtime. 4 discs. Audiophile AP–89/92.

PEMBERTON, BROOKE
The Ragtime Kid. Warner Bros. 1235.

PERLMAN, ITZHAK, AND ANDRÉ PREVIN
  The Easy Winners. Angel S–37113.

PIANO ROLL COLLECTIONS
  The Golden Age of Ragtime. Riverside RLP 12–110.
  Ragtime Piano Roll Classics. Riverside RLP 12–126.
  Scott Joplin Volume One. Biograph BLP–1006Q.
  Scott Joplin Volume Two. Biograph BLP–1008Q.
  Scott Joplin Volume Three. Biograph BLP–1010Q.
  Scott Joplin Volume Four. Biograph BLP–1013Q.
  Scott Joplin Volume Five. Biograph BLP–1014Q.
  Parlor Piano. Biograph BLP–1001Q.
  The Piano Roll. Folkways RBF–7.
  Piano Roll Ragtime. Sounds 1201.
  Pianola Jazz. (England) Saydisc SDL–117.
  Pianola Ragtime. (England) Saydisc SDL–132.
  James Scott Volume One. Biograph BLP–1016Q.
  The World's Greatest Piano Rolls. Dot DLP–25321.
  Volume Four. Dot DLP–25478.
  Picture Rags. (England) Transatlantic TRA SAM–26.

POLAD, MIKE
  The Cascades. Jazzology JCE–77.

PRYOR, ARTHUR
  Too Much Mustard. (England) Saydisc SDL–221.

PUFFER, TED, AND THE UTAH STATE UNIVERSITY CHORALE
  Treemonisha. Portents 3.
  The Queen City Jazz Band. Toad TR–LP2.

THE RAGTIMERS
  Play the Entertainer. RCA Camden ACL 1–0599.

RASCH, CHARLIE
  Ragtime down the Line. Ragtime Society RSR–4.
  Messin' Around. CK Records 8301–3900.
  Runnin' Wild. CK Records AR–3204.
  The Red Garter. Society Bear Records M670.

RESER, HARRY
  Banjo Crackerjax. Yazoo L–1048.

RIFKIN, JOSHUA
  Piano Rags by Scott Joplin. Nonesuch H–71248.
  Volume Two. Nonesuch H–71264.
  Volume Three. Nonesuch H–71305.

ROBERTS, LUCKEY
  Rent Party Piano. (England) RPP–1002.
  Harlem Piano. Good Time Jazz M–12035.
  Piano Ragtime of the Forties. Herwin 403.

ROBERTS, WILLIAM NEIL
  Great Scott. Klavier KS–510.
  Volume Two. Klavier KS–516.

ROGERS, ERIC
  Great Scott. London SPC–21105.

ROSE, WALLY
  Live from the Dawn Club. Fairmont 102.
  Ragtime Classics. Good Time Jazz M–12034.
  Rose on Piano. Blackbird C–12007.
  The Music of Jelly Roll Morton. Columbia 559.
  Cakewalk to Lindy Hop. Columbia 782.
  Ragtime Classics. Good Time Jazz L–3 (10").
  Ragtime Piano Masterpieces. Columbia CL–6260 (10").

RYAN, SLUGGER
  Plays Honky Tonk Piano. Judson J–3015.

THE SAINT LOUIS RAGTIMERS
  The Saint Louis Ragtimers. Audiophile AP75.
  Volume Two. Audiophile AP81.

SAN FRANCISCO HARRY
  Thirty Barbary Coast Favorites. Fantasy 3270.

SHEA, TOM
  Classic and Modern Rags. (Canada) Ragtime Society RSR–1.
  Prairie Ragtime. (Canada) Ragtime Society RSR–2.

SHIELDS, ROGER
  The Age of Ragtime. Turnabout TV S–34579.

SIGNORELLI, FRANK
  Ragtime Duo. Kapp KL–1005.

SMITH, WILLIE THE LION
  Original Compositions. Commodore 30.003.
  The Lion. (France) Vogue LD–693–30; GNP Crescendo GNPS–9011.
  The Legend. Grand Award GA 33–368.
  The Lion Roars. Dot DLP–3094.

Pork and Beans. Black Lion BLP–30123.
Grand Piano. Exclusive S–501.
The Memoirs. RCA LSP–6016.
Reminiscing the Piano Greats. Dial 305 (10″).
Live at Blues Alley. Halcyon 104.
California Here I Come. Flying Dutchman FD–10140.
Piano Ragtime of the Teens, Twenties and Thirties. Herwin 402.
Jazz Piano Greats. Folkways FJ–2852.
Harlem Piano. Good Time Jazz M–12035.
The Lion and the Tiger. (France) Jazz Odyssey 006.
And the Madelon. (France) Jazz Odyssey 009.

THE SOUTHLAND STINGERS
Palm Leaf Rag. Angel S–36074.
Magnetic Rag. Angel S–36078.

SPEAR, SAMMY
Authentic Ragtime Music. Mercury 20116.
Oh You Kid. Jubilee JLP–1110.

STONE, CHRIS
Gatsby's World—Turned On Joplin. ABC X–823.

SULLIVAN, JOE
Joe Sullivan Piano. Folkways FA–2851.
Swing Classics. Prestige 7646.

SUTTON, RALPH
Bix Beiderbecke Suite. Commodore FL 30.001.
Piano Solos. Riverside RLP 12–212.
Piano Ragtime of the Forties. Herwin 403.
A Salute to Fats. Harmony HL–7019.
Backroom Piano. Verve MGV–1004.
Ragtime U.S.A. Roulette R–25232.
Knocked-Out Nocturne. Project 3 PR–5040–SD.

THE TEMPERANCE SEVEN
The Temperance Seven Family Album. Parlophone PMC 1236.

THOMPSON, BUTCH
Plays Jelly Roll Morton. Center CLP–4.
Volume Two. Center CLP–9.

THOMPSON, CHARLES
Golden Reunion in Ragtime. Stereoddities C–1900.
Piano Ragtime of the Forties. Herwin 403.

TICHENOR, TREBOR
    Mississippi Valley Ragtime. Scroll 102.
    King of Folk Ragtime. Dirty Shame 2001.
    They All Play Ragtime. Jazzology JCE–52.
    Treemonisha. Deutsche Grammaphone 2707–083.

TRYFOROS, BOB
    Scott Joplin. Puritan 5002.

TURNER, RAY
    Honky Tonk Piano. Capitol T–188.
    Kitten on the Keys. Capitol H–306 (10″).

VAN BERGEYK, TOM
    Famous Ragtime Guitar Solos. Kicking Mule 114.

VAN EPS, FRED
    Kings of the Ragtime Banjo. Yazoo L–1044.

VAN RONK, DAVE
    Ragtime Jug Stompers. Mercury MG–20864.

WALDO, TERRY
    The Piano of. Fat Cat's Jazz FCJ–151.
    Snookums Rag. Dirty Shame 1237.
    Waldo's Gutbucket Syncopators. GHB 55.
    Jazz in the Afternoon. Blackbird C12009.
    Ohio Theater Concert. Blackbird C6002.
    Eubie Blake and His Proteges. Eubie Blake Music EBM–8.
    The New Black Eagles on the River. Dirty Shame Records 2002.

WATTERS, LU
    Bunk and Lu. Good Time Jazz L–12024.
    1942 Series. Good Time Jazz L–12007.
    Dawn Club Favorites. Good Time Jazz L–12001.
    Watters' Originals and Ragtime. Good Time Jazz L–12002.
    Stomps, Etc. and the Blues. Good Time Jazz L–12003.
    Blues over Bodega. Fantasy 5016.
    Live from the Dawn Club. Fairmont 101.
    Yerba Buena Jass Band Volume One. Homespun H–101.
    Volume Two. Homespun H–102.
    Unissued Live Recordings from Hambone Kelly's. Homespun H–103.
    Volume Four. Homespun H–104.
    Volume Six. Homespun H–106.

WEIDOEFT, RUDE
    George Olsen and His Music. RCA LPV–549.

WELLSTOOD, DICK
  Dick Wellstood Alone. Jazzology JCE–73.
  From Ragtime on. Chiaroscuro 109.
  Plays Ragtime Music of the Sting. Pickwick SPC–3376.
  Walkin' with Wellstood. (England) 77 Records SEU–12/51.
  Live at the Cookery. Chiaroscuro CR 139.

WHITCOMB, IAN
  Ian Whitcomb's Mod, Mod, Music Hall. Tower T 5042.
  Under the Ragtime Moon. United Artists UA–LA021–F.

WHITE, ALBERT (GASLIGHT ORCHESTRA)
  Your Father's Moustache Volume One. Barbary Coast 33002.
  Your Father's Moustache Volume Two. Barbary Coast 33008.
  Your Father's Moustache Volume Two. Fantasy 8040.

WILLIAMS, BERT
  American Vaude and Variety Volume Two. Rococo 4009.

WILLIAMS, QUENTIN
  Ragtime Piano. (England) Saydisc SDL–118.

WYNDHAM, TEX
  He's a Rag Picker. Fat Cat's Jazz FCJ–168.

ZIMMERMAN, RICHARD
  Scott Joplin, The Entertainer. Olympic 7116.
  Scott Joplin, His Complete Works. Murray Hill 931079.

ZINN'S RAGTIME STRING QUARTET
  Zinn's Ragtime String Quartet. Music Minus One CJ–13.

Bibliography

BOOKS

Bierley, Paul E. *John Philip Sousa: American Phenomenon.* Englewood Cliffs: Prentice Hall, 1973.

Blesh, Rudi. *Combo: U.S.A.: Eight Lives in Jazz.* Philadelphia: Chilton Book Co., 1971.

Blesh, Rudi, and Harriet Janis. *They All Played Ragtime: The True Story of an American Music.* 4th ed. New York: Oak Publications, 1971.

Bolcom, William, and Robert Kimball. *Reminiscing with Sissle and Blake.* New York: Viking Press, 1973.

Charters, Ann. *Nobody: The Story of Bert Williams.* New York: Macmillan Co., 1970.

Cuney-Hare, Maud. *Negro Musicians and Their Music.* Washington: Associated Publishers, 1936.

Doctorow, E. L. *Ragtime.* New York: Random House, 1975.

Ewen, David. *History of Popular Music.* New York: Barnes and Noble, 1961.

Freedland, Michael. *Irving Berlin.* New York: Stein and Day, 1974.

Goldberg, Isaac. *Tin Pan Alley: A Chronicle of the American Popular Music Racket.* New York: John Day Co., 1930.

Henri, Florette. *Black Migration: Movement North, 1900–1920.* Garden City, N.Y.: Anchor Press, 1975.

Jasen, David A. *Recorded Ragtime: 1897–1958.* Hamden, Conn.: Archon Books, 1973.

Jones, LeRoi. *Blues People: The Negro Experience in White America and the Music That Developed from It.* New York: William Morrow and Co. 1963.

Laufe, Abe. *Broadway's Greatest Musicals.* New York: Funk and Wagnalls, 1969.

Lomax, Alan. *Mister Jelly Roll.* New York: Grosset and Dunlap, 1950.

Marks, Edward B. *They All Sang: From Tony Pastor to Rudi Vallée.* New York: Viking Press, 1935.

McLuhan, Marshall. *Understanding Media: The Extensions of Man.* New York: McGraw-Hill, 1964.

Mellers, Wilfred. *Music in a New Found Land: Themes and Developments in the History of American Music.* London: Barrie and Rockliff, 1964.

Newley, I. A., ed. *The Development of Segregationist Thought.* Homewood, Ill.: Dorsey Press, 1968.

Nketia, J. H. Kwabena. *The Music of Africa.* New York: W. W. Norton and Co., 1974.

Parkes, Henry Bamford. *The United States of America: A History.* Rev. ed. New York: Alfred A. Knopf, 1959.

Rose, Al. *Storyville, New Orleans: Being an Authentic, Illustrated Account of the Notorious Red-Light District.* Alabama: University of Alabama, 1974.

Schafer, William J., and Johannes Riedel. *The Art of Ragtime: Form and Meaning of an Original Black American Art.* Baton Rouge: Louisiana State University Press, 1973.

Schechter, William. *The History of Negro Humor in America.* New York: Fleet Press, 1970.

Shacter, James D. *Piano Man: The Story of Ralph Sutton.* Chicago: Jaynar Press, 1975.

Shapiro, Nat, and Nat Hentoff. *Hear Me Talkin' to Ya.* New York: Dover Publications, 1955.

Southern, Eileen. *The Music of Black Americans: A History.* New York: W. W. Norton and Co., 1971.

Stearns, Marshall. *The Story of Jazz.* New York: Oxford University Press, 1959.

Stoddard, Tom, ed. *The Autobiography of Pops Foster, New Orleans Jazzman.* Berkeley/Los Angeles/London: University of California Press, 1973.

Whitcomb, Ian. *After the Ball.* Middlesex: Penguin Books, 1972.

Williams, Martin T., ed. *The Art of Jazz: Essays on the Nature and Development of Jazz.* New York: Oxford University Press, 1959.

Williams, Martin T., ed. *Jazz Panorama: From the Birth of Dixieland to the Latest "Third Stream" Innovations—the Sounds of Jazz and the Men Who Make Them.* New York: Collier Books, 1964.

Witmark, Isadore. *The Story of the House of Witmark: From Ragtime to Swing Time.* New York: L. Furman, 1939.

ARTICLES

"About Ragtime." *Christensen's Ragtime Review* II-8 (August 1916): 12.

Arneson, Bruce and Tom Arneson. "The Roy Bargy Story." *Rag Times* VI-3 (September 1972): 8–10.

Belt, Byron. "Ragtime Great's Opera Disappoints Reviewer." *Times-Picayune*, August 20, 1972.

Bethell, Tom. "The Revival of Bunk Johnson." *Mississippi Rag*, II-9 (July 1975): 1–3.

"Best Songs Never Make Hits." *Christensen's Ragtime Review*, I-6 (June 1915): 12.

Bolcom, William and Robert Kimball. "The Words and Music of Noble Sissle and Eubie Blake." *Stereo Review*, November 1972, pp. 56–64.

Brockhoff, Dorothy. "Missouri Was the Birthplace of Ragtime: Widow of Music Publisher Recalls Legendary Scott Joplin and How His Music Took Country by Storm." *St. Louis Post Dispatch*, January 1961.

Brooks, John. "A Novel in Ragtime: What Doctorow Is after Is Magic." *Chicago Tribune*, July 6, 1975.

Cable, George Washington. "Creole Slave Songs." *Century Magazine* XXX-84 (April 1886).

Cable, George Washington. "The Dance in Place Congo." *Century Magazine* XXXI-52 (February 1886).

Cassidy, Russ. "Joseph F. Lamb: A Biography." *Ragtime Society Newsletter* IV-1 (January 1965): 4–5.

Charters, A. R. Danberg. "Negro Folk Elements in Classic Ragtime." *Ethnomusicology: Journal of the Society for Ethnomusicology* V-3 (September 1961): 173–183.

Charters, Samuel, "Ragtime—Pristine and Pre-*Sting*." *New York Magazine*, July 15, 1974, p. 57.

Christensen, Axel. "Tone and Touch for Ragtime." *Christensen's Ragtime Review* I-7 (July 1915): 5–6.

Coe, Richard L. "Two Works at Once Old and 'New' at the Kennedy Center." *Washington Post*, September 14, 1975.

Collier, James Lincoln. "The Scott Joplin Rag." *New York Times Magazine*, September 21, 1975, pp. 18–33.

Curtis, Olga. "The Ragtime Music of Max Morath." *Ragtimer* VI-5/6 (final issue 1967): 4–8.

Darch, Robert R. "'Blind' Boone: A Sensational Missourian Forgotten." *Ragtimer* VI-5/6 (final issue, 1967): 9–13.

Daugherty, Jane. "Ragtime Revival Makes Sense to Knocky." *St. Petersburg Times*, November 6, 1974.

Davin, T. "Conversations with James P. Johnson." *Jazz Review* II (June 1959): 14–17.

Davis, Peter G. "*Treemonisha*—An Innocent Dream Come True." *New York Times*, June 1, 1975.

Dreyfuss, Joel. "A Rescue of Ragtime: 'Perfectly Made Music.'" *Washington Post*, June 16, 1975.

Dunning, Jennifer. "Louis Johnson: 'I Love Dance—Any Kind of Dance.'" *New York Times*, September 28, 1975.

Ekwueme, Lazarus E. N. "African-Music Retentions in the New World." *Black Perspective in Music* II-2 (Fall 1974): 128–144.

Harrah, Madge. "The Incomparable Blind Boone." *Ragtimer*, September/October 1973, pp. 4–8.

Hentoff, Nat. "Piano Playing that Sings." *New York Times*, July 29, 1973.

"HGO's Objective for *Treemonisha*: Authenticity." Publicity release by Houston Grand Opera reprinted in *Rag Times* x–2 (July 1975): 1.

"In Retrospect: Black Musicians in Early Ethiopian Minstrelsy." *Black Perspective in Music* III-1 (Spring 1975): 77–99.

Jasen, David A. "Ragtime Explained." *Storyville* 37 (October 1, 1971): 4–7.

Jasen, David A. "Zez Confrey: Creator of the Novelty Rag." *Rag Times* V-3 (September 1971): 4–5.

"Joe Jordan (1882–1971)." *Rag Times* V-4 (November 1971): 1.

Johnson, Leslie Carole. "A Popular History." *Mississippi Rag* III-1 (November 1975): 1–2.

Johnson, Leslie Carole. "Bunk in Brief." *Mississippi Rag* II-9 (July 1975): 3.

Johnson, Leslie Carole. "Rifkin on Ragtime." *Mississippi Rag* II-5 (March 1975): 1–3.

Johnson, Ron D. "Max Morath: Living a Ragtime Life." *Mississippi Rag* I-12 (October 1974): 6–7.

Jones, Robert. "The Seduction of Frank Corsaro by Joplin's 'Treemonisha.' " *New York Times*, September 21, 1975.

Kramer, Karl. "Blow the Horn! *Treemonisha* is Reborn!" *Ragtime Review* IV-4 (October 1965): 8–9.

Kramer, Karl. "Influence of Ragtime on Stage Music." *Ragtime Society Newsletter* IV-1 (January 1965): 4–5.

Kramer, Karl. "*Treemonisha*: Its Place in American Opera." *Ragtimer*, September/October 1973, pp. 4–8.

Kronenberger, John. "The Ragtime Revival: A Belated Ode to Composer Scott Joplin." *New York Times*, August 11, 1974.

Kupferberg, Herbert. "Joplin's Opera Finally Makes It Big." *National Observer*, September 27, 1975.

Lampe, J. Bodewalt. "The Art of Arranging Music." Reprinted in *Rag Times*, January 1974, from an article in the 1917 issue of *Tuneful Yankee*.

Larkin, Arthur D. "Does Ragtime Spoil the Classical Student?" *Christensen's Ragtime Review* I-7 (July 1915): 12.

Lewis, Claude. "Too Often Monetary Rewards Go Elsewhere." *Philadelphia Bulletin*, December 8, 1974.

McKay, Blythe. "Ragtime Music Written in Macon Object of Search." *Macon Telegraph*, August 3, 1962.

Montgomery, Michael. "An Open Letter from Mike Montgomery." *Jazz Report* VI-6.

Morath, Max. "Up from Ragtime." *Variety*, January 5, 1966.

Nadel, Norman. "Ragtime Emerges as a 'Hot Property.' " *Columbus Citizen-Journal*, September 3, 1974.

Pleasants, Henry. "*The Art of Ragtime*: A Book (and a Subject) Reviewed." *Stereo Review*, September 1974.

Powers, Frank, "Ragtime Stock Orchestrations." *Ragtime Society News-letter* V-5 (November 1966): 44–50.

"Ragtime at the Indianapolis Fair." *Christensen's Ragtime Review* I-8 (August 1915): 14.

"Ragtime Opera." *Newsweek*, February 7, 1972, p. 46.

"Ragtime Sweeps the Nation." *Rag Times* V-5 (January 1972): 1.

Reed, Addison W. "Scott Joplin, Pioneer." *Black Perspective in Music* III-1 (Spring 1975): 45–52; Parts III-2 and III-3 (Fall 1975): 269–277.

Rich, Alan. "Premonitions of 'Treemonisha.'" *New York Magazine*, September 8, 1975, pp. 57–58.

Rogers, Charles Payne. "Charles Thompson: Ragtime Pioneer." *Ragtimer* VI-1 (April 1967): 8.

Saal, Hubert. "Glad Rags." *Newsweek*, August 5, 1974, p. 59.

Saal, Hubert. "Joplin's Black Gold." *Newsweek*, September 22, 1975, pp. 62-63.

Schafer, William J. "'Fizz Water': Ragtime by Eubie Blake, Luckey Roberts and James P. Johnson." *Mississippi Rag* III-2 (December 1975): 1–2.

Schonberg, Harold C. "Music: 'Treemonisha.'" *New York Times*, January 31, 1972.

Schonberg, Harold C. "Scholars, Get Busy on Scott Joplin." *New York Times*, January 24, 1971.

Schuller, Gunther. "Scott Joplin's Operatic Vision Comes to Life." *New York Times*, May 18, 1975.

Shea, Tom. "Finney's Orchestra." *Ragtime Society Newsletter* IV-4 (July/August 1965): 34–38.

Southern, Eileen. "Afro-American Musical Materials." *Black Perspective in Music* I-1 (Spring 1973): 24–32.

Thacker, Eric. "Ragtime Roots." *Jazz and Blues* III-9 (December 1973): 4–6.

Thompson, Butch. "Buying Ragtime Music." *Mississippi Rag* I-8 (June 1974): 11.

Tichenor, Trebor. "Chestnut Valley Days: An Interview with Charlie Thompson." *Ragtime Review* II-2 (April 1963).

Tichenor, Trebor. "'Ham and I': A Rare Sort of Classic Rag." *Ragtime Review* V-1 (January 1966): 9.

Tichenor, Trebor Jay. "Missouri Ragtime Revival." *Rag Times* IV-4 (November 1970): 1–2.

"Treemonisha." *New York Times*, December 15, 1974.

"Treemonisha in Atlanta." *Rag Times* V-5 (January 1972): 1.

"Treemonisha on Broadway." *Rag Times* IX-4 (November 1975): 1–3.

Trombley, William. "Traditional Jazz Alive, Well in S.F." *Los Angeles Times*, April 26, 1975.

Vanderlee, Ann, and John Vanderlee. "Scott Joplin's Childhood Days in Texas." *Rag Times* VII-4 (November 1973): 5–7.

Viertel, Jack. "Scott Joplin: His Rags, Whose Riches?" *New Times*, November 29, 1974, pp. 55–58.
Voche, Warren. "Dick Wellstood." *International Musician*. January 1976.
Wadler, Joyce. "Marvin Hamlisch: Three of a Kind." *New York Post*, 1974.
Waterman, Guy. "A Survey of Ragtime." *Record Changer* XIV (1955): 7–9.
White, John Alfred. "A Dialogue on Ragtime." *Mississippi Rag* I-10 (August, 1974): 2–3.
"Will Ragtime Save the Soul of the Native American Composer?" *Current Opinion* LIX (December 1917): 406–407.
Wilson, Olly. "The Significance of the Relationship Between Afro-American Music and West African Music." *Black Perspective in Music* II-1 (Spring 1974): 3–22.
Zimmerman, Dick. "*Treemonisha* Charms the Critics." *Rag Times* V-6 (March 1972): 7.

MUSIC COLLECTIONS

Bert Williams Folio of Ne'er-to-be-Forgotten Songs. New York: Robbins-Engel, 1925.
Blesh, Rudi, ed. *Classic Piano Rags.* New York: Dover, 1973.
Charters, Ann, ed. *The Ragtime Songbook.* New York: Oak Publications, 1965.
Exciting Era of Zez Confrey, The. New York: Belwin/Mills, 1963.
Freemont, Robert A., ed. *Favorite Songs of the Nineties.* New York: Dover, 1973.
Golden Encyclopedia of Ragtime from 1900 to 1974. New York: Charles Hansen Educational Music and Books, 1974.
Jackson, Richard, ed. *Piano Music of Louis Moreau Gottschalk.* New York: Dover, 1973.
James P. Johnson's Piano Jazzfest. New York: Bregman, Vocco and Conn, 1946.
Jazz Master, The: A Collection of Famous Piano Solos by Billy Mayerl from the Golden Age of Jazz. New York: Keith Prowse Music Publishing Co., 1972.
Lawrence, Vera Brodsky, ed. *The Collected Works of Scott Joplin.* 2 vols. New York: New York Public Library, 1971.
Levy, Lester S., ed. *Sousa's Great Marches in Piano Transcription.* New York: Dover, 1975.
Meares, Dick and David LeWinter, eds. *Piano Solos by James P. Johnson.* New York: Clarence Williams Music Publishing Co., 1946.
Morath, Max, ed. *Max Morath's Giants of Ragtime.* New York: Edward B. Marks, 1971.
Morath, Max, ed. *One Hundred Ragtime Classics.* Denver: Donn Printing, 1963.

Morath, Max, ed. *Ragtime Guide: A Collection of Ragtime Songs and Piano Solos.* 2d ed. New York: Hollis, 1964.
Play Them Rags: A Piano Album of Authentic Rag-Time Solos. New York: Mills Music, 1961.
Rag Classix. New York: Warner Brothers, 1973.
Ragtime Piano: A Collection of Standard Rags for Piano Solos. New York: Belwin/Mills, 1963.
Ragtime Treasures by Joseph F. Lamb (Piano Solos). New York: Mills Music, 1964.
Shealy, Alexander, ed. *World's Favorite Music and Songs: Ragtime Piano.* New Jersey: Ashley Publications, 1973.
Strictly "Rags": Memory Lane in Rag-time (A Vocal-Piano Collection). New York: Remick Music, 1960.
Tichenor, Trebor Jay, ed. *Ragtime Rarities: Complete Original Music for Sixty-three Piano Rags.* New York: Dover, 1975.
Waldo, Terry, ed. *Sincerely, Eubie Blake: Nine Original Compositions for Piano Solo.* New York: Edward B. Marks, 1975.
Whitcomb, Ian, ed. *I Remember Ragtime.* New York: Charles Hansen Educational Music and Books, 1974.
Whitcomb, Ian, ed. *Tin Pan Alley: A Pictorial History (1919–1939) with Complete Words and Music of Forty Songs.* New York: Paddington Press, 1975.

RECORD LINER NOTES

Affeldt, Paul E. Notes on *Vintage Piano Volume Three.* Euphonic ESR 1203.
Blesh, Rudi. Notes on *Scott Joplin: The Complete Works for Piano.* RCA CRL5-1106.
Bolcom, William. Notes on *William Bolcom: Heliotrope Bouquet: Piano Rags, 1900–1970.* Nonesuch H-71257.
Charters, Samuel B. Notes on *Joseph Lamb: A Study in Classic Ragtime.* Folkways FG-3562.
Colt, Stephen. Notes on *David Jasen: Fingerbustin' Ragtime.* Blue Goose BG 3001.
Elwood, Phillip. Notes on *Lu Watters' Yerba Buena Jass Band: Unissued Live Recordings from Hambone Kelly's.* Homespun H-103.
Grinstead, Dan. Notes on *The Music of Joe Jordan.* Arpeggio ARP-1205.
Hentoff, Nat. Notes on *Harlem Piano.* Good Time Jazz M-12035.
Hill, George Roy. Notes on *The Sting.* MCA 390.
Kimball, Robert E. Notes on *The Eighty-six Years of Eubie Blake.* Columbia C2S-847.
Koenig, Lester. Notes on *Lu Watters' Yerba Buena Jass Band Volume One.* Good Time Jazz L-12001.

Koenig, Lester. Notes on *They Tore My Playhouse Down*. Good Time Jazz L-12025.

Montgomery, Michael. Notes on *Scott Joplin—1916: Classic Solos Played by the King of Ragtime Writers and Others from the Rare Piano Rolls*. Biograph BLP-1006Q.

Rust, Brian. Notes on *Too Much Mustard*. Saydisc SDL 221.

Wellstood, Dick. Notes on *Dick Wellstood Alone*. Jazzology JCE-73.

Index

Other DACAPO titles of interest